C000160589

I really like Sharon's book. I like
and applies one important verse. I
memorisation. I like that it feels r
kind of thing written by someone
all, I like it because it helped me grow as a Christian and be more
like the Saviour that both Sharon and I love.

Adrian Reynolds

Pastor, author and Associate National Director, Fellowship of
Independent Evangelical Churches

This book packs a ton of wisdom, help, and humor into a small
space. Sharon does a great job showing that when we understand
God's love, it transforms us so that we look more like Jesus. As
I read, I found myself challenged and helped to be more loving,
joyful, patient, and gentle. I plan to use this book with a new
Christian this week!

Mike McKinley

Senior Pastor, Sterling Park Baptist Church, Virginia

CHARACTER

HOW DO I CHANGE?

SHARON DICKENS

SERIES EDITED BY MEZ McCONNELL

CHRISTIAN
FOCUS

Copyright © Sharon Dickens 2019
paperback ISBN 978-1-5271-0101-2
epub ISBN 978-1-5271-0486-0
mobi ISBN 978-1-5271-0487-7

10 9 8 7 6 5 4 3 2 1

Published in 2019
by
Christian Focus Publications Ltd,
Geanies House, Fearn, Ross-shire,
IV20 1TW, Great Britain.

www.christianfocus.com
Cover and interior design by Rubner Durais

Printed and bound
by Bell & Bain, Glasgow

CONTENTS

PREFACE

The only time I remember going to church as a family was weddings. Even then my dad would wait outside until we were finished. I did occasionally go to a local children's Sunday school where I learnt a few Bible stories. At school we had an assembly every Friday, old school hymns (which I now love) and a nice thought for the day from the local minister. I learned to recite the Lord's Prayer of by heart – I had to say it every Friday for 7 years. I didn't really understand any of this, it was just something we had to sit through without laughing or getting caught talking to your friends. It was years before someone actually explained the gospel to me.

As a new believer I didn't have a clue what 'being a real Christian' looked like. For a young Christian there seemed to be lots of voices and not all of them telling me the most helpful of things. That's why the 'Voices' book in this series is so important – I had to learn which voice to listen to and which to ignore.

It was confusing. People would tell me what being a Christian was suppose to look like. So much seemed to matter – what I wore, the Bible I used, the way I talked, the words I used, my personality (being feisty was definitely the first thing that would have to change). Everyone had something to say about something. I felt like a square peg in a round hole and it seemed like I was going to have to change everything about myself. Was this really what God expected?

Thankfully, a mature godly women called Marjory got alongside me. She helped me unravel what the Bible had to say about these things. I realised over time that most of the things that Christians told me were elements of a Godly character were in fact cultural, not biblical. It was just the way they liked a Christian to look – like them. It took me a long time to realise that I was to conform to the standard Jesus set out, and not some idealistic, twee, vanilla image that some Christians think of as Godly.

In this book, I hope to – just like my friend Marjory did for me – help you unravel what the bible has to say about a Godly Character: what Jesus' standards are for your life.

Sharon Dickens
July 2019

SERIES INTRODUCTION

The First Steps series will help equip those from an unchurched background take the first steps in following Jesus. We call this the 'pathway to service' as we believe that every Christian should be equipped to be of service to Christ and His church no matter your background or life experience.

If you are a church leader doing ministry in hard places, use these books as a tool to help grow those who are unfamiliar with the teachings of Jesus into new disciples. These books will equip them to grow in character, knowledge and action.

Or if you yourself are new to the Christian faith, still struggling to make sense of what a Christian is, or what the Bible actually says, then this is an easy to understand guide as you take your first steps as a follower of Jesus.

There are many ways to use these books.

+ They could be used by an individual who simply reads through the content and works through the questions on their own.

+ They could be used in a one-to-one setting, where two people read through the material before they meet and then discuss the questions together.

+ They could be used in a group setting where a leader presents the material as a talk, stopping for group discussion throughout.

Your setting will determine how you best use this resource.

A USER'S KEY:

As you work through the studies you will come across the following symbols …

JACKIE – I'm going to introduce you to Jackie. There will be times in each chapter when you'll hear something about her story and what's been going on in her life. We want you to take what we've been learning from the Bible and think about what difference it would make in Jackie's life and our own. So, whenever you see this symbol you'll hear a bit more about what's going on with her.

ILLUSTRATION – Through real-life examples and fake scenarios, these sections help us to understand the point that's being made.

STOP – When we hit an important or hard point we'll ask you to stop and spend some time thinking or chatting through what we've just learnt. This might be answering some questions, or it might be hearing more of Jackie's story.

KEY VERSE – The Bible is God's Word to us, and therefore it is the final word to us on everything we are to believe and how we are to behave. Therefore we want to read the Bible first, and we want to read it carefully. So whenever you see this symbol you are to read or listen to the Bible passage three times. If the person you're reading the Bible with feels comfortable, get them to read it at least once.

MEMORY VERSE – At the end of each chapter we'll suggest a Bible verse for memorisation. We have found Bible memorisation to be really effective in our context. The verse (or verses) will be directly related to what we've covered in the chapter.

SUMMARY – Also, at the end of each chapter we've included a short summary of the content of that chapter. If you're working your way through the book with another person, this might be useful to revisit when picking up from a previous week.

MEET JACKIE

Jackie is a single mum to three young children. She is in her mid-thirties and has lived in a Glasgow housing scheme all of her life. She was with her partner Frank for over ten years but six months ago he left her. Jackie has three kids: Jake (11), who has a different dad from Billee-Jean (8) and wee Frankie (3). Her oldest boy, Jake, doesn't see his real dad at all as he did a bunk the minute he found out Jackie was pregnant. In fact, Jake sees Frank as his dad. Frank never treated him any differently from his own two kids. Frank has tried to see the kids, but when they do see him the meeting usually turns into a screaming match between him and Jackie over money and visitation rights. Jackie has been struggling to bring up the kids and coping with life since Frank left her. She's tired all the time, sick of constantly trying to make ends meet and feels the pressure of always having to make the decisions. She wants her life to change but she just doesn't know how that is going to happen.

LIFE NOW

Jackie was first introduced to the Christian message at Sunday School when she was a child, but her life took a different turn in her early teens. She appeared at a church Christmas carol service after receiving an invitation through the door. After that she started coming to practically every Sunday service, and loved singing hymns and listening to the Bible being taught. Her kids also started coming to the clubs and Sunday School. It wasn't long before she accepted the good news of Jesus, put her faith in his finished work, and asked Him to come and change her messed-up life.

But there's a problem: since then, her life doesn't seem to have changed that much from Monday to Saturday. She fights with neighbours (too noisy at night), she is forever getting into trouble on Facebook (her family is annoying and often 'two-faced'), and the Social Services are always checking up on her and the children. When asked, she would say she is a Christian, but would recognise that her life does not match up to her profession of faith. She wants to change but she's not really sure that she can ever truly change or where to start. She feels hopeless, especially when she looks at some of the women at church – they all seem so perfect to her.

This is Jackie's story …

WHAT'S THE POINT?

Christians should grow in love.

1. ALL WE NEED IS LOVE, RIGHT?

Sitting in a café one day people-watching, I spied a couple having lunch. It was hard to miss that they were together – the matching jumpers creepily screamed 'we're an item' – but it wasn't the only resemblance. When I looked closer they actually looked similar. It's odd, right, but have you noticed that the longer you spend with someone you like, the more you seem to take on some of their characteristics and mannerisms? It starts with the odd word here and there and before you know it you're finishing their sentences and coordinating outfits. We are influenced and changed by our time with those we love. It should be the same for us as Christians.

As we spend time with God and grow in maturity, we should be influenced by Him and become more and more like Jesus.

It's a bit of a weird thought to get your brain around, but as Christians we actually have the Spirit of God, the Holy Spirit, living in us. Now common sense tells us that if He's living in us, there should be some evidence of that in our lives. He is bound to influence us. I'm not talking surface influence like suddenly having a deep desire to wear a checked shirt, carry a large Bible and have a WWJD friendship bracelet (What Would Jesus Do) on your left wrist … *Jesus bling*. I mean our character! Having the Spirit dwell in us has got to have an impact on our character, and we should see evidence of that in our lives.

STOP

So, as a professing Christian what should Jackie's life look like?

'I love those who love me, and those who seek me find me. With me are riches and honour, enduring wealth and prosperity. My fruit is better than fine gold; what I yield surpasses choice silver. I walk in the way of righteousness, along the paths of justice, bestowing a rich inheritance on those who love me and making their treasuries full' (Prov. 8:17-21).

Sometimes people describe the evidence of God's presence in our lives as 'fruit'. Just like my wee mum sees the evidence of the healthy apple tree in the crop of juicy apples she collects from her garden, we would expect any Christian to grow and produce 'fruit' in their lives.

In this book we are going to look at the 'fruit' that should be evident in our lives as Christians: the fruit of the Spirit.

STOP

Do you think that all the fruit we see in our life is good fruit?

'But the fruit of the Spirit is **love**, *joy, peace, forbearance, kindness, goodness, faithfulness, gentleness and self-control. Against such things there is no law'* (Gal. 5:22-23).

Have you ever seen the cartoon strip of a man and woman wearing fig leaves with the caption 'Love is …'? Love is never having to say you're sorry, love is always having someone to hold hands with, love is saying I love you at random moments, love is soothing away all his worries … *really?!* When we think of love, lots of us think of romance, all hearts and flowers. It's that way you feel, the butterflies inside, when they look at you from across a room (and I'm not talking about indigestion!). We think love is all passion and sex. Our idea of love comes from movies, TV, fairy-tales …. At the movies we hear the sweeping music when he goes in for the first perfect kiss that lasts just long enough not to be weird. They don't awkwardly bump noses or stand on their toes as they move in and I'm sure their breath is minty fresh. It is after all, perfect; it's *love*. Is that what love is?

But we all know real life is not like the movies. The first kiss wasn't surrounded by music, and six months after you say 'I do' you realise the things you thought were cute little habits are just plain annoying. Just like Cinderella realised after she married Prince Charming, 'happily ever after' meant picking his underwear up off the bathroom floor just like everyone else. The person you married doesn't seem the same – when you were dating they couldn't do enough to please you, but now that you're married it's a different story. It's not how you planned it, and so you ask yourself, is this love?

Do we really understand what love is?

JACKIE

Jackie met Frank when she was round her pal Aggie's one night for a cuppa tea. She wasn't exactly looking that fabulous sitting in her pyjamas with her hair pulled back in a pony-tail, but she and Frank hit it straight off. He was funny. They never exactly went on a date or anything, but after he popped in for a cuppa tea the next night he just never seemed to go home. It was weeks before he said 'Love you, babe!'

STOP

What do you think 'love' is?

If we really want to understand what love is we need to look at the love of God. By understanding the love of God we will understand how to really love each other. If we look at 1 John 4:7-12 we will see what God's love looks like.

'Dear friends, let us love one another, for love comes from God. Everyone who loves has been born of God and knows God. Whoever does not love does not know God, because God is love. This is how God showed his love among us: He sent his one and only Son into the world that we might live through him. This is love: not that we loved God, but that he loved us and sent his Son as an atoning sacrifice for our sins. Dear friends, since God so loved us, we also ought to love one another. No one has ever seen God; but if we love one another, God lives in us and his love is made complete in us' (1 John 4:7-12).

The first bit we need to focus on is that love is sacrificial. Now the truth is, we aren't going to like that because, at the heart of all of us, is a selfish 'me' monster. If we are honest that's not how we see love playing out, is it? For many of us love is about getting something we want, not us sacrificing anything. Yet we can see clearly in verse 9 that God shows His love for us by sending His only Son so that we might love each other and Him the way we are supposed to, through Him. When we think about that a bit more we see that at the centre of God's love is sacrifice. He is giving up His Son; it is absolutely costly. Love is costly – it always involves us giving of ourselves to another person. That grinds against the little selfish 'me' monster who loves to get its own way. We need to be less self-serving and more self-giving. So, what does this look like?

 ILLUSTRATION

Jackie stepped off the bus and trudged along the road. It was raining heavily. *'PERFECT!'* she thought to herself. She's exhausted, some woman before her in the queue had a complete meltdown at the store assistant, and in the end they had to call the police. It took ages – if she hadn't desperately needed gas and electric she'd have left. It's been a totally horrendous day, she'd had another fight with Frank, she was soaking, the shopping bag handle had snapped, that stupid woman had made her late picking up the kids, and the whole walk home the kids were snapping at each other. She had a banging headache and the day wasn't even over yet. She was seething about Frank: 'All he does is play his stupid mind games.' Her brain was spinning as she went over and over yesterday's texts, re-reading them several times. 'One minute he's texting me saying I'm the only woman he ever really loved and how he's made a massive mistake, then I see him all over Mary outside the shop! I'm gonna smash her when I see her,' Jackie's thoughts raged on. 'Like I dunno what I saw – I can't believe the cheek of him telling me he was just chatting with her, like it was all in my head! I'll "all in my head" him, let's see how cocky he is when he doesn't get the kids this week – that'll wipe the smile off his face. He's an idiot and I'm done with him completely.' She seethed all the way up the road. She walked in the door, put the TV on, gave Jake some money for take-out and went straight to her bed.

Maybe every woman reading this illustration is completely hating Frank right now, and every bloke is saying what a psycho Jackie is and how Frank's well rid of her, but, nothing's ever that clear cut. Life and the truth are usually far more complicated than the snippet we see here. Jackie is claiming to be a Christian, however, and this should have an impact on how she deals with things.

STOP

Jackie is professing Christ but does that mean she just rolls over and takes Frank's nonsense? How do you think Jackie should have responded? How well is she loving Frank and the kids?

 'Do nothing out of selfish ambition or vain conceit. Rather, in humility value others above yourselves, not looking to your own interests but each of you to the interests of the others' (Phil. 2:3-4).

Think of the people in your life. Now how often is your love self-serving and selfish? Share an example.

We morph what we think about love with a little bit of truth, a lot of selfishness and bad habits that we have picked up along the way. We convince ourselves this is 'love'.

We twist it our own way. Our wrong thinking affects how we love those around us.

We see it in the mum who never says 'no' to her kid because she thinks that's how to show love or the husband who's controlling his missus because he thinks that protecting her.

There are actually thousands of examples of how we have twisted what love looks like. No matter how much we lie to ourselves, if we really think about it, our version of love isn't that helpful in the long-term to those we care about.

To understand what real love looks like, we need to look at what the Bible says and think through God's love. **Love is part of His being and His character.** As we think about God's love, what love really is, this will show us how to love others well.

Let's look more closely at these verses from 1 John 4.

 'This is how God showed his love among us: He sent his one and only Son into the world that we might live through him. This is love: not that we loved God, but that he loved us and sent his Son as an atoning sacrifice for our sins' (1 John 4:9-10).

I hinted at it earlier, but straightaway we can't miss what verse 9 says. God shows His love for us by sending His Son into the world so that we could be saved through Him. At the very centre of God's love we see that it is sacrificial, self-giving and costly.

That's mind-blowing when we think about it.

We don't even like giving up our place in the queue at a super-market for the wee old woman behind us with only three items in her basket, never mind making an *actual* costly sacrifice.

Wrap your brain around this. For eternity, Father, Son and Holy Spirit have been together in perfect love. Think of the loss they must have felt when God sent His only Son into the world for us. I know that Christmas cards look all lovely and our Easter cards are a PG-rated version of what really happened, but the truth we see in the Bible is very different. Jesus came to save a people who:

didn't particularly want Him,

weren't that thankful,

despised Him,

rejected Him,

humiliated Him

and eventually, after a brutal beating, crucified Him.

Yet God sent Him and Jesus obeyed. That's love, that's GREAT SACRIFICIAL LOVE! What we see Jesus do on the cross is die for the sins of His enemies. Romans 5:8 ESV says '… but God showed his love for us in that, while we were still sinners, Christ died for us.' That's a smack in the face to those of us who struggle to love those we actually care about, never mind our enemies. Now that's a step too far, I hear you say – you ask too much to love like that. But this is how God has loved us. Jesus made the ultimate sacrifice by paying the price we owed for our sin. He appeased God's wrath and turned it away from us. Why? Why would anyone, never mind God, do this for us? Because He loves us. His love shows us truly what love is. It is sacrificial and costly.

> **STOP**
>
> What do you think about the price that God paid for you? Do you think that it was too high a cost?

This should have an impact on our lives. We started this chapter thinking about God's love so we could understand it more and love better. 1 John 4:11 says, 'Dear friends, since God so loved us, we also ought to love one another.' When we understand God's love, we need to pause and think about how we are showing that kind of love to others. Love is not just a fluffy word, it's a real and active thing. We might even have to love people we find totally annoying and difficult (including that numpty who gets on your nerves – you know the one I'm talking about!).

> **STOP**
>
> How are you supposed to love those that drive you nuts?

If we're being honest, when it comes to those who drive us nuts, the character flaw that gnaws at us is usually something all too often evident in our own lives. In our heads we might be judging them for being an arrogant so-and-so but, if we look at our own hearts, chances are we are fairly arrogant ourselves. The problem is usually us. The mighty SELF monster has risen and is on the loose again. We need to deal with our own sinful attitudes first.

We need to recognise that love is often a choice.

I know that sounds odd but we need to choose to love others in the light of what Christ did for us. His love was costly and we too need to love at cost to ourselves. Not being self-serving, like Frank was in the illustration earlier, but self-giving. If Frank was really self-giving he'd be helping his wife clean and tidy up every day and not just when he wanted something. Just think about the impact that would have on his wife, his marriage and his family.

I think if we're being honest this is the hardest bit because it takes effort. We might have to do something we don't like. We might even have to give up something like our beloved coffee or a take-away on a Saturday night so we can support a church intern.

STOP

What's your worst-case scenario – what's the one thing you wouldn't do?

We need to get over ourselves and our comfort-loving, self-serving, selfish hearts and look to what Jesus did on the cross for us. When we learn to love like Jesus, 1 John 4 tells us that God's love is shown in the world through us. People see that it's different, and it says something to them. It's part of how we witness that God is real in our lives; we share a bit of who God is through the way we love others.

In this book we are thinking about how God is evident in our lives. Jesus says that the world will know that we are His disciples by the way we love one another. Would they see real love if they looked at our lives? What do we need to change to make that more evident to those around us?

KEY POINT

Love is … to give ourselves sacrificially for the benefit of others just as Christ has done for us.

MEMORY VERSE

'This is love: not that we loved God, but that he loved us and sent his Son as an atoning sacrifice for our sins. Dear friends, since God so loved us, we also ought to love one another' (1 John 4:10-11).

SUMMARY

We have the wrong idea about love. Most of the time we think it's about our feelings or even romance. But real love isn't exactly what we think. Jesus modelled real love for us when He sacrificially died for us. We need to look at Jesus as our example and like Him, sacrificially love people instead of just worrying about ourselves.

WHAT'S THE POINT?
Christians should grow in joy.

2. WE'RE LITTLE BUNDLES OF JOY, RIGHT?

'Joy is the serious business of heaven.' – C. S. Lewis

 *'But the fruit of the Spirit is love, **joy**, peace, forbearance, kindness, goodness, faithfulness, gentleness and self-control. Against such things there is no law'* (Gal. 5:22-23).

The other week I was listening to a programme on the radio talking about mental health issues in young people. It suggested that a quarter of all mental health issues start in childhood. I have to say that freaked me out a little, so I did what everyone does when they don't believe something: I googled it. After a quick search I found an article that said that children of depressed parents have a 50 per cent risk of developing depression before age twenty. This wasn't getting any better the further I looked.

But then I realised that I wasn't really that surprised. I see the reality of this every day and it's sad. Life is hard. People are depressed, anxious, hopeless and stressed. Their dreams are squashed and they are seriously struggling. For some these feelings seem to be so overwhelming that they are consumed by it and feel that there is just no escape. Others battle on and try to deal with it. But how do they do that, and what is it they really want?

If you ask most people what they want, deep down, it would be 'to be happy'. In fact, if most of us with kids were asked the same question, we would say, without blinking, the same thing: 'We want our kids to be happy'. We just have to flick through magazines and watch TV for five minutes to see how advertisers take advantage of that – everything they sell will make you happy and is the answer you are looking for. They tell us that the next holiday, a new sofa for Christmas, losing 20 kilos, the latest trainers, whiter teeth, laser eye treatment, a bigger TV, the new breakfast cereal that will have you skipping down the road singing, or that must-have, new-fangled gadget is just what we need to satisfy and make us happy.

 JACKIE

Jackie spent too much time worrying about what everyone thought of her and the kids. There just never seemed to be two pennies to rub together, but she always managed to make sure the kids got what they wanted and had the best of clothes and gadgets. Every time she bought something new Frank was happy because she was a genius at bargain-hunting – she always seemed to be in the right place every time. 'I love my kids to be happy – they have to have what they want.'

We all know these temporary things make us *happy* for a moment, but we also know it's fleeting and won't last. Sadly, many lives are filled with deep sadness and nothing that truly resembles happiness. There is an emptiness and no joy at all. The world and this stuff can provide temporary relief, but it doesn't get to the heart of the matter. Only when we start thinking through what the Bible has to say about what joy is will we start to understand. The Bible shows us that in chasing temporary happy fixes, we are chasing the wind and pursuing the wrong things.

 'Yet when I survey all that my hands had done and what I had toiled to achieve, everything was meaningless, a chasing after the wind; nothing was gained under the sun' (Eccles. 2:11).

As we have been learning, having God in our lives should change who we are and what people see. The evidence is the fruit in our lives. Galatians 5:22-23 tells us that we should have joy.

The Bible makes it clear that, as Christians, joy should be seen in our lives – it should be normal for us.

It's supposed to be a reality of our faith in Christ. But how does that work when everything around us is kicking off? I know it's hard to wrap our brains around, but even when life is kicking us in the teeth we should be able to feel joy. That might sound warped and twisted, but maybe as with 'love', we don't really understand what the Bible means when it talks about joy.

STOP

Do you think joy is different from happiness?

We confuse happiness with joy all the time because they seem similar. But, as I've said, happiness is based on our temporary circumstances. Like when our team scores a goal, we get a pay rise at work, we find money in the street, we get asked out on a date, we get news that our friend has had a baby, or when we've gone a bit wild and had our hair dyed pink and it looks sharp. Our happiness is based on the things around us. It can all change with the next goal the other side score, a notice of redundancy, a break-up, or a bad haircut …. Suddenly we're gutted and happiness seems a thing of the past.

But joy isn't like that.

It's different.

Joy, true biblical joy, isn't fleeting; it doesn't budge or change no matter what life throws at us. Joy lasts.

JACKIE

I don't get how that's possible. What is joy then?

Joy is delighting in God no matter what.

Biblical joy is steadfast and lasts because it isn't based on what's going on around us or how we feel that day. Instead it's found in God and He never changes. When we define what biblical joy is we have to look beyond the temporary things and get to the heart of the matter – to our hearts. Our hearts, our souls, our very being have been changed by the gospel. As we have said before, the fruit of joy should be in our lives as evidence of our transformation in Christ and our salvation.

 'Though you have not seen him, you love him; and even though you do not see him now, you believe in him and are filled with an inexpressible and glorious joy' (1 Pet. 1:8).

Peter describes it as an inexpressible and glorious joy. If I'm being honest, when we look at some Christians today, they don't look like they are filled with an inexpressible and glorious joy. They look gloomy, like they've just lost a million pounds or have been slapped across the face with a wet fish. Sometimes I think there are people who seem to actually get *joy* out of being a crabby moaning-faced complainer. They have this austere, dour, stony-faced look about them that would chill a cup of tea. It's not the best witness. Why would that attract anyone to Christ?

If biblical joy is missing from a Christian's life, then that's like a spiritual siren going off, wailing 'there's something wrong'. Hear me right, I'm not saying we should fake it either – pasting a big cheesy smile on our face and telling everyone 'I'm fine' when our world is crashing about our ears isn't helpful either. No matter the circumstances in a Christian's life there should be joy in the gospel of Christ.

If joy is missing, there's a reason.

I'd be asking 'How's your quiet time?' 'Are you neglecting God?' 'Are you reading and thinking about His Word?' 'Are you praying?' 'Or is there disobedience or unrepentant sin?' 'What's God asking you to do, or convicting you of, that you're ignoring?'

> **STOP**
>
> Do you feel like giving up? Is that 'No Joy Siren' wailing in your ears? Ask yourself – why? Why is my joy missing?

Believe me, no matter what's going on and how much life is kicking us about, there is one thing that is still the same, unchanging – the gospel. If we are true followers of Christ then we are forgiven and our salvation is solid and that should put joy in our hearts.

 ILLUSTRATION

There once was a man called Horatio Spafford. He lived many years ago. If we were writing a script for a disaster movie we could use his life as our storyline. So much happened to him. His son died at two years old, he lost all his money and was bankrupted by the great Chicago fire. Soon after the fire he decided he and his family would visit friends in England. He booked them all passage on a ship called *Ville Du Havre* but, at the last minute, business delayed him and he sent his family on without him. During the voyage there was a devastating collision between two boats and both sank quickly. It was carnage. His wife was the only one who survived.

All this sounds like something we would find in the Old Testament book of Job. Who could even imagine how Horatio felt? How would we cope with something like that? Yet as he sailed to meet his wife, crossing the ocean that had claimed his children, he wrote the song 'It is Well with My Soul'. He found his joy in the gospel of Christ and delighted in God, **no matter what.**

JACKIE

I get whingy and think the world has come to an end if we've run out of milk and I can't have a cup of tea, never mind facing something like this bloke. I would be devastated if something happened to my kids. I remember when little Frankie fell down the stairs and broke his leg I was completely useless; Frank had to take him to hospital without me. I don't understand how this bloke can find joy when his family is dead. That's gotta be wrong – it's impossible!

'Therefore, since we have been justified through faith, we have peace with God through our Lord Jesus Christ, through whom we have gained access by faith into this grace in which we now stand. And we boast in the hope of the glory of God. Not only so, but we also glory in our sufferings, because we know that suffering produces perseverance; perseverance, character; and character, hope. And hope does not put us to shame, because God's love has been poured out into our hearts through the Holy Spirit, who has been given to us' (Rom. 5:1-5).

In the book of Romans, we see Paul's reaction as everything life could muster was thrown at him. He was beaten and slung into jail, he was shipwrecked, there were days he didn't have enough food to eat, he was rejected by his own people, and he struggled with long-term ill health. Basically, in the scale of life sucking, Paul was ranking higher than most! Yet when he wrote Romans 5, we see Paul rejoicing, having joy in God no matter what is happening to him. Paul was constantly thankful for the gospel. He knew that no one could take away his salvation, that he was 100 per cent forgiven, and that fueled his joy. He knew God was in control and that was enough for him – he totally trusted Him. His hope was in Jesus.

STOP

Can we say the same? What do you think that means for us as we live day to day?

Becoming a Christian isn't like some sort of magic genie version of religion. We can't say something three times, rub our hands together and make it all go away. What we can do, though, when the dark days come, is remember the promises we have in Christ and preach the gospel to ourselves. We can remind ourselves that God's promises are true and trust Him.

Cling to Him and don't lose hope!

Whatever is going on, whatever life throws at us.

However overwhelming, however heartbreaking, you can still find rest in Christ. It may even feel like the weight of it is crushing you, but you can still find true joy in Him. He will hold us fast. We can trust Him.

 'So we do not lose heart. Though our outer self is wasting away, our inner self is being renewed day by day. For this light momentary affliction is preparing for us an eternal weight of glory beyond all comparison, as we look not to the things that are seen but to the things that are unseen. For the things that are seen are transient, but the things that are unseen are eternal.' (2 Cor. 4:16-18, ESV).

We must not forget what is to come: eternity with the God who saved us. We may have put our hope in temporary things that make us happy for five minutes, but we know deep down that they are fleeting. 2 Corinthians reminds us that the temporary things don't remotely compare to the glory that is to come in eternity. We may be broken, battered and bruised by life, but this life is the temporary thing.

STOP

Why do you struggle to find joy in your life? How can you cling to Christ more?

No matter what, we can find our joy in the gospel of Christ and delight in Him. When we do, we too can sing, and mean it, 'It is well, it is well with my soul.'

KEY POINT

We find our joy when we delight in God, no matter what. Remember the hope we have in Christ and cling to Him. Don't lose hope.

 ## MEMORY VERSE

'Blessed be the God and Father of our Lord Jesus Christ! According to his great mercy, he has caused us to be born again to a living hope through the resurrection of Jesus Christ from the dead, to an inheritance that is imperishable, undefiled, and unfading, kept in heaven for you ...' (1 Pet. 1:3-4, ESV).

or

'I saw the Holy City, the new Jerusalem, coming down out of heaven from God, prepared as a bride beautifully dressed for her husband. And I heard a loud voice from the throne saying, "Look! God's dwelling place is now among the people, and he will dwell with them. They will be his people, and God himself will be with them and be their God. He will wipe every tear from their eyes. There will be no more death or mourning or crying or pain, for the old order of things has passed away."' (Rev. 21:2-4).

SUMMARY

All too often we confuse happiness and joy because they are so similar. Happiness is based on temporary things, like the circumstances of life. So, when good things happen we are happy but when disaster falls upon us we are crushed by it. Unlike happiness, joy is something that doesn't change depending on the circumstances. Biblical joy lasts when we delight in God no matter what's going on around us.

WHAT'S THE POINT?

Christians should grow in peace.

3. GIVE PEACE A CHANCE

'*But the fruit of the Spirit is love, joy, **peace**, forbearance, kindness, goodness, faithfulness, gentleness and self-control. Against such things there is no law*' (Gal. 5:22-23).

JACKIE

Walking home through the park last week I spotted Jackie dragging one of her kids behind her. She was seriously stressed. I could tell, even from a distance, that her whole body was bristling with anger. She shouted to her pal walking down the road and then the picture became clearer: she'd lost her little girl, Billee-Jean. I felt so sorry for her. Anyone with kids knows that feeling; the fear, the dread, the anxiety, all overwhelm you as you scan every inch of the area hoping to spot the familiar sight of your child. Then her mobile rang and without even a pause, she screamed down the phone. It was BJ. Jackie was raging at her. She had gone from blind panic to blind rage in a millisecond – she was screaming and dragged wee Frankie behind her in the other direction. I'd hate to have been BJ when she got home.

Too many of us are fuelled by anger. We're righteously annoyed at someone or something. The kids who are driving us mad, the welfare worker who stopped our benefits, friends on Facebook that have cheesed us off, that guy who cut us up in traffic. The list is endless. Sometimes it seems that most people walk around with a low-level anger buzzing around them and it really doesn't take a lot before they are flying off the handle at the latest tiny annoyance. Volatile and dangerous, they are weighed down with, and exhausted by, the torrent of emotion raging within.

For so many of us peace seems like a fantasy, something we are never going to achieve in our lifetime. If we google 'peace', scan magazines, look at books on Amazon or even flick to the right TV adverts, they are all full of tips and 'how to' guides for finding inner peace. It seems like everyone and their granny is in search of peace. But are they all searching for the same thing? Some people think peace is just not having an argument for five minutes or not mouthing off at the doctor's receptionist. Others think that peace is having no hardship in life, not having a care or a worry, or no war in the world. So what is peace?

STOP

If I asked you, what would you say peace is?

I love that scene in the movie *Miss Congeniality* when the beauty pageant contestants are all asked, 'What's the most important thing society needs?' One by one, over and over, they all smile sweetly and say the same thing: 'World peace!', followed by a massive round of applause and a few whoops from the audience. Then Sandra Bullock's character, Gracie Hart, steps up to the microphone. It's her turn to answer the question. She hears the question, 'What's the most important thing society needs?' All poise and grace, she answers, 'That would be harsher punishment for parole violators, Stan …' There's a stunned silence and all we can hear is crickets chirping in the background. Stan looks awkward and doesn't know quite what to do until finally Gracie adds, ' … aaaaand World Peace!' The crowd goes wild with applause. 'World Peace' might be the imagined standard answer at a beauty pageant, but what is this peace they all seem to want?

Most people would define peace as the absence of war, being calm all the time or living a life free from any hassle, struggles or chaos.

But is it just that?

If so, then how can we understand Bible verses that tell us that trouble and strife should be expected in our Christian life? For example, James 1:2-3 (ESV) says 'Count it all joy, my brothers, when you meet trials of various kinds, for you know that the testing of your faith produces steadfastness.' That little word 'when' that we see in verse 2 tells us that, as Christians, we should expect trials and struggles in our lives.

So can peace really just be the absence of hassles and struggles?

How does that work if, as a Christian, we are to expect trials but we are also to have peace in our lives? Confusing, right? There has to be more to it than that. So what is it then?

How do I get it?

How do I get peace with other people and for myself?

Am I actually supposed to have peace anyway if you're telling me I'm supposed to expect struggles and hard times?

All these questions could make our brains melt if we aren't careful. They can feel a bit overwhelming. But lets start to think some of this through. Hopefully by the end of this chapter we will have a better understanding of both what peace is and what it looks like in our lives.

 'Therefore, since we have been justified through faith, we have peace with God through our Lord Jesus Christ' (Rom. 5:1).

Romans tells us that peace goes beyond just living without strife, that it's more than just the absence of conflict or inner turmoil. It talks about a peace that can only come from knowing that everything is settled and sorted with God. Romans tells us our greatest need is to have peace with God, and we can only find that peace through His Son Jesus.

> **STOP**
>
> Why would we not have peace with God in the first place?

Our relationship with God was ripped apart because of sin. We've ignored God, rebelled against Him and basically done our own thing. In fact, He can't even look at us, we are so detestable to Him. **Habakkuk 1:13 says 'Your eyes are too pure to look on evil; you cannot tolerate wrongdoing.'** Our sin is an affront to a holy and perfect God, and we need protection for fear of being totally consumed in His presence. Getting the picture? It's not a good one, right, and not remotely a peaceful one!

'There is no one righteous, not even one; there is no one who understands, there is no one who seeks God. All have turned away' (Rom. 3:10-12).

Romans 3:20 says, 'No one will be declared righteous in God's sight by the works of the law; rather, through the law we become conscious of our sin.'

We have broken God's law and that comes at a price.

The law is there to show us what God is like and at the same time, it shows us what we've become, because we can't keep it. It points us to Christ and our need for Him. Like a mirror reflects back the reality of what we look like, the law gives us a glimpse of who we truly are. Basically, we are not just up a creek, we are in the middle of a tsunami, without a paddle. But before you have a complete meltdown – there's good news. Now I know I took a long time getting there, but I can promise, it's worth the wait.

We can't keep the law,

but Jesus could and did.

'I have told you these things, so that in me you may have peace. In this world you will have trouble. But take heart! I have overcome the world' (John 16:33).

Outside of Jesus we can never find true peace. It's as simple as that. There is no way we can remotely defend ourselves or pay the price our sin demands. Without Christ the tsunami of God's judgments would totally and justifiably wipe us out. *But,* God gave us an out. He chose to save us through Jesus Christ.

 'For Christ also suffered once for sins, the righteous for the unrighteous, to bring you to God' (1 Pet. 3:18).

 ILLUSTRATION

You're at Jackie's for a cup of tea and her ex-partner, Frank, comes up in the conversation. Soon she is telling you why he really left. She tells you about getting a letter in the post one day saying she's being taken to court for not paying the credit card, and now with all the interest and the court charges the debt is in the thousands. For months and months, she'd been ignoring the demand letters, shoving them in the kitchen drawer, hoping Frank never found them, and suddenly she's faced with a debt that has more zeros than she knew existed. She thought she was going to lose everything, and they even found out she'd actually been committing fraud. Now it was about more than the money: she was potentially facing criminal charges. She eventually had to confess and tell Frank, and he went completely ballistic. 'I swear I actually thought he might hit me at one point, but he smashed that hole through the wall instead,' she says, pointing to her living room wall. 'All we did was argue for weeks. It was exhausting dealing with the fear, the hassle, and I just kept crying all the time. Now I have to go to court on my own. Frank doesn't care about anyone but himself.' The truth was out. Frank left because he couldn't cope with all her lies, the manipulation or the fighting. It was too much even now for her to admit – it was easier to be angry at him.

The court date came quicker than she expected and you go along for moral support. You know no matter how remorseful or how smart she looks in your aunt's best suit, there is nothing good going on in her favour. At best she's getting a massive fine and having to pay it all back. 'I hate this place. It's like everyone is staring at me. I'm feeling sicker and sicker.' Seeing her lawyer in the corner, Jackie is slightly confused because he seems proper chuffed. This made her angry because this had been one of the worst days of her life. When he's talking she doesn't seem to understand him at all. To be honest, you're finding it hard to believe the truth yourself. But here's what he said: an anonymous person paid the debt in full this morning including the court costs. 'Couldn't have been Frank – who would do that? Nah, that's not right. He's got to be playing some sort of sick game with my head. Debt-free and they are dropping the charges – how is that even possible?'

No illustration is perfect, but this is how Jesus bought our peace with God through His death. Perfect and sinless, He paid the price we should have, becoming sin for us. Romans 5:19 says, 'For just as through the disobedience of the one man [Adam] the many were made sinners, so also through the obedience of the one man [Jesus] the many will be made righteous.' In paying our debt, not only did Jesus satisfy God's judgment, but we're made righteous. God not only forgives us because Christ paid for our sins – He also treats us as if we actually never sinned. What I mean is that He treats us as if we have perfectly obeyed God's law. Don't be fooled, He's not actually ignoring our sin; the cost has to be paid, but by Christ. He paid the price and bought us everlasting peace with God. The tsunami becomes as quiet and gentle as a duck pond.

STOP

Go back to Jackie's story. Stand in Frank's shoes for a minute – she's been hiding all the debt and fraud from you, signing your name and getting you into debt. How would you have reacted? Could you forgive her? How should Jackie have handled it as a new believer?

I've said so many times in previous chapters that when we become Christians we should change. When we find peace with God through Christ – we should change. We see this in our lives, because not only has our relationship with God changed and been restored, but our relationships with others also change. Not only can we have peace with God, but we can have peace with people too. We see the evidence of this change when we start to practise forgiveness and patience, we fight the temptation to whine and moan, we actually take responsibility for our sin instead of blaming something or someone else, we resist the urge to be self-righteous and judgmental, or when we fight our pride. Suddenly we notice the way we were living and don't want to live like that anymore. God is transforming us.

When we are transformed from the inside out we stand out, people notice, and God is glorified.

I feel at this point I should write 'the end' and we should walk away high-fiving ourselves because we've 'been justified through faith, we have peace with God through our Lord Jesus Christ' (Rom. 5:1). All sorted, end of story, right? I mean, God is steadfast and never changing. Nothing can change the peace we have with Him now, right? But what if that's not true for us? What if right now, there's no peace in my life?

STOP

Is there something robbing you of your peace? What is it?

Is it unrepentant sin? Like Jackie, are you lying to those around you? Got your feet stuck in two camps? Lusting after something or someone you shouldn't be? Secretly 'at it' on the sly? Not trusting God? Worrying about everything? Being a total control freak? Is the pain of your past affecting your present? Are you relying on and trusting in the wrong things?

 'There is now no condemnation for those who are in Christ Jesus' (Rom. 8:1).

The thing with truth is that we all too easily forget it. It's like we learn a lesson and bang, three minutes later we've completely forgotten it. We constantly have to be reminded of the truths of the gospel and speak them into our lives. Whatever is robbing you of your peace, run to God in prayer and repentance. Be honest with Him and cling to Him, giving thanks for your salvation and the hope we have in Christ. He bought our peace through the blood of Jesus and no one but us, with foolish disobedience and sinfulness, can steal that away.

KEY POINT

Jesus bought our peace through the blood of Jesus and only our foolish disobedience and sinfulness can destroy our peace.

 MEMORY VERSE

'Rejoice in the Lord always. I will say it again: Rejoice! Let your gentleness be evident to all. The Lord is near. Do not be anxious about anything, but in every situation, by prayer and petition, with thanksgiving, present your requests to God. And the peace of God, which transcends all understanding, will guard your hearts and your minds in Christ Jesus' (Phil. 4:4-7).

SUMMARY

Peace seems to be something that we are all striving for, never achieving or even understanding. Peace is more than just living without conflict and strife. We need to experience the peace that comes from knowing that everything is settled and sorted with God. Through His death, Jesus brings us peace with God. Outside of Jesus we will never find real peace.

WHAT'S THE POINT?

Christians should grow in patience.

4. DON'T PUT THE CART BEFORE THE HORSE: PATIENCE

 *'But the fruit of the Spirit is love, joy, peace, **forbearance**, kindness, goodness, faithfulness, gentleness and self-control. Against such things there is no law'* (Gal. 5:22-23).

When I was a kid we had a prime minister called Maggie Thatcher. Anyone in the UK who's older than eighteen will know who she is. She was beloved by the suburbanites and loathed by the working class. Thatcher was like Marmite, you either loved her or hated her; there was no middle ground. So this is a first for me, and I know for sure it's going to be the last, but I want to quote the Iron Lady herself. 'I am extraordinarily patient, provided I get my own way in the end.'

> **STOP**
>
> What do you think she was actually saying?

The trouble is, Thatcher hit the nail on the head. Many of us define patience as just waiting until we get what we want – but that's not really being patient, is it? That's just being stubborn, immovable or showing an iron will. Sadly, we can take this kind of thinking into our relationship with God. We ask God for something and then just wait for Him to deliver the goods like He's Amazon. In fact, we want Him to deliver like Amazon Prime (now or next day)! Then when we don't get what we want, the way that we want it, we have a crisis in our faith, a meltdown, a tantrum! We might even question if God really loves us. After all, if He really loved us He would have given us what we wanted in the first place, right?! We grumble and moan about the situation and ultimately we start grumbling and moaning about the Lord.

Patience is not just about waiting for something or even waiting 'well' for the coveted thing; it's so much more. To understand the depth of the word *patience*, we need to first think about the patience that God shows us. We need to think about patience as a characteristic of God, how He models patience to us, and what that means for us as Christians.

Biblical patience is God exercising restraint because of His love and mercy for sinful man. As sinners we are fully deserving of His wrath, but He holds it back, for a time. He shows restraint. He exercises patience with us so that we may repent and be restored to Him. That's a bit different to what we've been thinking, isn't it? More than just us waiting until we get our Amazon wish list, isn't it?

We see examples of God's patience all over the Bible, but here are a couple of examples:

'For many years you were patient with them. By your Spirit you warned them through your prophets. Yet they paid no attention, so you gave them into the hands of the neighbouring peoples' (Neh. 9:30).

'What if God, although choosing to show his wrath and make his power known, bore with great patience the objects of his wrath – prepared for destruction? What if he did this to make the riches of his glory known to the objects of his mercy, whom he prepared in advance for glory – even us, whom he also called, not only from the Jews but also from the Gentiles?' (Rom. 9:22-24).

God's patience is long but it's not infinite; it will come to an end.

He has already appointed a day in which He will judge the world. That day will mark the end of God striving in patience with us. So basically, He's patient now, but it's not going to last forever. It's going to end and we need to be ready for what's to come.

God holding back judgment day so we can all hear the gospel isn't the only way He shows us His patience. God shows His patience with us as we change and grow.

I feel like a broken record because I keep saying the same thing over and over again. Having Christ in our life should impact our lives, and we should start to display His characteristics – characteristics like patience. I am not naturally the most patient person in the world, and I've struggled writing this because the truth has been hard to escape. **But patience isn't optional for the Christian.** We'd like to think it is because it's difficult, but it isn't. God is patient and we are commanded to be patient also.

JACKIE

When I watch the church women on Sunday it's like they are Mary Poppins. Their kids never seem to kick off like my kids. It's easier for them to be patient with their kids than me with mine. No matter what I do, they just won't do what I say, but I'm really trying. It's not easy.

STOP

How do you react when someone has annoyed you or upset you? Do you hold back when you're angry or upset, or do you let it rip?

'Put on then, as God's chosen ones, holy and beloved, compassionate hearts, kindness, humility, meekness, and patience, bearing with one another ...' (Col. 3:12-13, ESV).

How do you display the same patience that God shows you? What does that look like for you?

We actually have to apply this to our day-to-day lives and be patient with one another. Knowing that we need patience and actually displaying it are two different things.

I know that's when we become unstuck.

When we are under pressure, what comes to the surface is the real us. You know what I mean: the 'real you', that side of you that you've been reining in or hiding in case anyone sees. The you that appears in those moments when you're tired and stressed at the kids as they get on your last nerve. Our patience wears thin and our irritation levels go through the roof. When the pressure comes fast and furious, the first thing that goes out the window is our patience. In fact, many of us don't even need that much to set us off because we've all got those little things, our pet hates, the things that rile us up and send us over the edge quicker than usual. For those things we don't even need the excuse of pressure to see the irritation levels rise and our patience dissipate.

For me it's checkout queues. I'm seriously impatient at the checkout and it's worse when the assistant is being a complete idiot, taking ages to do the simplest of tasks, and has to ring the bell for help every three minutes. BUT, no matter how big the queue, how late I'm running, how clueless the assistant is, there is no excuse for me losing my rag and being impatient. Now, I don't actually lose my rag these days, but I know I can be fairly formidable when I'm annoyed, and if I leave that unchecked I can be intimidating.

STOP

What makes you mad and sends you over the edge?

ILLUSTRATION

Hanging out with Jackie one day, we nipped into the supermarket for a few quick things when I saw a sign saying 'Keys cut in two minutes'. We needed keys cut and thought 'Perfect, two birds with one stone.' I stood in the queue and told the assistant I wanted three copies of the same key cut. What proceeded was twenty minutes of the assistant making constant mistakes, rebooting the machine, and staring at the screen saying 'Ermmm, I don't know what to do.' She asked two people and started the key-cutting process five times. With every ounce of my being I stood there trying to remain calm, struggling to find the patience to stand and wait. So much time had passed that I actually started to assess whether I should stay or just go. But by then I knew I was invested: I had to hang it out, and Jackie was watching.

Eventually another assistant came and took over and I got my three keys five minutes later. 'I'm sorry,' the new assistant said, at which point Jackie chipped in: 'I hope you're better than that blooming idiot. I'm growing old waiting for her to stop messing about!' The assistant looked a bit red and said, 'I'm so sorry, I don't know what she did to the machine.' Me neither! I might have pulled off looking patient, I may have looked all serene and muttered something trite like 'no worries', **but** I wasn't. I was feeling exactly like Jackie; inside I was seriously raging.

STOP

Is there really any difference between my behaviour and Jackie's?

We all like to think we are masters at concealing our feelings, but no matter how hard we try, impatience and frustration will have tell-tale signs. We will in some way give ourselves away – every nerve will be itching to say 'I'm getting seriously angry'. Here's the problem: we are impatient. Far too often grace can go quickly out the window in those everyday moments. Like when our son's lost his school shoe for the second time that week and it's always just the one, when that crazy dude cuts us up on the bypass and just waves as he passes, when we go to the fridge and someone has used the last of the milk and put the empty bottle back in the fridge … we say in frustration, 'really?!' In these moments we too easily forget the grace that we have been shown and get frustrated, irritated and impatient.

We are frustrated with people instead of gracious.

Impatient instead of patient.

In these moments we overlook the fact that they are our Christian family and rarely think about our witness to those who don't know Christ – **we turn people into targets for our frustration.** No matter how hard we try, our impatience is hard to hide.

 'But I received mercy for this reason, that in me, as the foremost, Jesus Christ might display his perfect patience as an example to those who were to believe in him for eternal life' (1 Tim. 1:16 ESV).

I remember saying to my son when he was little, 'How many times do I have to tell you?' and he, taking my question literally, said without any sass intended, 'I don't know, seven?' That made me laugh for ages and reminds me that God says the same thing to me regularly: 'Sharon, how many times do I have to tell you?' We can become all self-righteous and forget how many times we've messed up. How many times have we got things wrong? How many times has God had to teach us something again and again? And yet God shows us His immeasurable patience and kindness. This is more than we deserve and definitely more than we show others.

People aren't all we can get impatient with. There are times when we can be impatient with God and His timing. As Christians we use the term 'to wait well'. What we mean by this is that we are sure of God's will and we are waiting well on His perfect timing. But we are the McDonald's generation – not only do we not like waiting, we also don't like to hear 'no' – we want it and we want it now.

There is a perfect example of what we are like in the movie *Willy Wonka and the Chocolate Factory* (the *original* of course). The character Veruca Salt sings the song 'I want it now! ... I don't care how, I want it now!' This pretty much sums it up for many of us. 'I don't care how, I want it now.' When we don't get what we want when we want it, we somehow make it happen. We force the issue and we get ourselves in a right mess. We're too impatient to wait on God's perfect timing.

I've seen this with single men and women who are desperate for a relationship. Don't get me wrong, the desire to be married is good, a gift from God. But I have spoken to many women who simply aren't ready to wait or are tired of waiting. They don't trust God or His timing. They can easily get depressed and upset because it feels like everyone is in a couple except for them. They feel incomplete, discontent, left on the shelf and anxious. Having a relationship has become an idol (it's more important to them than God is). Their loneliness and desperation for a husband fuels their decisions and they start to make bad choices. People can easily rush into a relationship and even allow themselves to get sexual very quickly, crossing lines they never would have contemplated before. Perhaps they even choose someone who really isn't a mature Christian, or make that choice to go out with a non-Christian (date to save!). They tell themselves the lie that obviously dating a Christian will force their boyfriend to see their desperate need for salvation (Aye, right!). All of this can lead to children out of wedlock, women considering abortions, painful breakups, struggling marriages or even Christians walking away from the Lord.

We forget that God is wise. We forget that God is faithful. We forget that God actually knows what He is doing. We forget to wait and trust. **We forget to be patient.**

STOP

What are you constantly asking God for or always talking to Him about? How would you feel if God said no?

I remember once as a young Christian praying for something and being reminded by someone that God uses the waiting to change us. I never really appreciated that at the time; I just thought it was too hard and unrealistic to patiently wait. When we are struggling to be patient we need to remember the grace that Jesus has shown us and patiently wait upon His promises. We need to look to Him, rely on Him and ask Him to help us as we struggle to show patience. Thankfully Christ is infinitely patient with us.

KEY POINT

God has patience but it's not infinite. His patience will come to an end. He's appointed a day when He will judge the world, marking the endpoint of God striving in patience with us. We are called to be patient – it isn't optional for us – but it's hard! Thankfully we have a Saviour who gives us all that we need, even patience.

MEMORY VERSE

'Blessed be the God and Father of our Lord Jesus Christ! According to his great mercy, he has caused us to be born again to a living hope through the resurrection of Jesus Christ from the dead, to an inheritance that is imperishable, undefiled, and unfading, kept in heaven for you ...' (1 Pet. 1:3-4 ESV).

SUMMARY

Many of us are impatient, we want something and we want it now. Patience isn't just about us waiting for something or showing restraint. Patience is an alien concept for us but, not for God. God patiently holds back His judgment so that we can repent and return to Him, restored. But we must remember His patience isn't infinite; at some point it will come to an end. For the Christian patience isn't an optional extra. We are to bear with one another, growing in and showing patience, following the example set before us by God.

WHAT'S THE POINT?

Christians should grow in kindness.

5. WE CATCH MORE FLIES WITH HONEY

 *'But the fruit of the Spirit is love, joy, peace, forbearance, **kindness**, goodness, faithfulness, gentleness and self-control. Against such things there is no law'* (Gal. 5:22-23).

By now you will probably realise that I love movies. I feel like I've started what could easily become a habit of always having at least one movie quote in a chapter, but I know that will too easily distract me and divert my focus as I search my memory banks for any useful scene. When I think of kindness, though, there is one movie that just pops into my brain – etched there as a classic. *Pay it Forward*. I challenge anyone to watch that movie without weeping. A young boy called Trevor attempts to make the world a better place after his teacher gives his class an assignment. The assignment is to think of something that can change the world and then put it into action. Trevor comes up with the idea of paying a favour forward – to think up three 'significant' good deeds to do for people (strangers) and then actually put them into practice. Then the person receiving the deed needs to 'pay it forward' and do three significant deeds for others. Trevor's efforts to make good on his idea trigger a revolution not only in his own life but also for his alcoholic grandmother, the emotionally scarred teacher, and eventually a whole nation as 'Pay it Forward' becomes big news and he ends up being interviewed by the media. People just love a good story!

But it's not just in the movies we see random acts of kindness. Google 'random acts of kindness' and there are over 1,580,000 results; in fact, there is even a 'random acts of kindness day' to celebrate on the 17th February. There is everything from dogs being rescued by strangers to people having their restaurant bill paid for them, pages and pages of teary-eyed stories of real-life acts of kindness from strangers. I loved the one about an old woman who left her waiter a huge tip, alongside a handwritten note. It read, 'Luke, the tip for you was given because you reminded me of my son, Devon, who died fifteen years ago. Maybe you look a little like him, but it is your kind, gentle, conscientious mannerly spirit that makes the connection. Thanks for the bittersweet memory. God bless you, dear!'

JACKIE

Wee Doris is eighty-two and has lived in the flat under Jackie for years. Every time Jackie makes a pot of soup she sends one of the kids down with a tub full for Doris. Even now Frank still gets her bread on a Saturday morning when he's getting his papers and leaves them hanging on her door handle. Wee Doris is a doll and everyone knows her.

One thing that struck me about all the stories and quotes is simply that most, if not all, acts of kindness, provoke gratitude. The waiter was so happy not only with the sweet note but with the massive tip; the dog owner was thrilled and hugged the man who dived into the ocean to save her dog; and the homeless lady who got her meal paid for showed her gratitude by buying a meal for someone else when she got her life sorted.

But imagine how the guy would have felt after he stripped to his waist and jumped in the freezing water to rescue the dog if, after this act of heroism, the owner gave him nothing but cheek and anger or didn't even acknowledge him. He'd be a bit irritated, right? I mean, we get annoyed when we give way to another car and the driver doesn't acknowledge our kindness. No wave, no flashing hazard lights – nothing. We are irritated, right? We expect there to be gratitude after a kindness shown and we are thrilled if they gush!

> **STOP**
>
> How do you feel if you do something kind for someone and they don't say thanks?

However, God's kindness is different. His kindness is unaffected by the gratitude or ingratitude of those to whom it's shown. God's kindness isn't influenced by the outcome or the response of the recipient. We see that in Luke 6:35.

'But love your enemies, and do good, and lend, expecting nothing in return, and your reward will be great, and you will be sons of the Most High, for he is kind to the ungrateful and the evil' (Luke 6:35 ESV).

This is a freaky thought, right?! We have heard over and over that we are to be Christ-like and display His characteristics in our lives. Yet here we see God showing mercy and kindness to His enemies, to the ungrateful and evil! Thinking about being kind to people we like is easy for us to get our heads around. Being kind to the ungrateful is annoying, but even though we might struggle with that, I don't think many of us would actually stop being kind because of it. But being kind to our enemies and to the evil?! No way, surely that's a step too far.

 ILLUSTRATION

The Christian Corrie ten Boom and her sister Betsie were arrested for concealing Jews in their home during the Nazi occupation of Holland. They were sent to a concentration camp. Corrie wrote her story in her autobiography, *The Hiding Place*.

She describes the day she meets her former guard, the enemy, after the war. It happened after she had finished giving a talk at a church in Munich about God's forgiveness. She writes,

> And that's when I saw him …. It came back with a rush: the huge room with its harsh overhead lights, the pathetic pile of dresses and shoes in the center of the floor, the shame of walking naked past this man. I could see my sister's frail form ahead of me, ribs sharp beneath the parchment skin … this man had been a guard at Ravensbrück concentration camp where we were sent.
>
> Now he was in front of me, hand thrust out: 'A fine message, fräulein! How good it is to know that, as you say, all our sins are at the bottom of the sea!'
>
> And I, who had spoken so glibly of forgiveness, fumbled in my pocketbook rather than take that hand. He would not remember me, of course – how could he remember one prisoner among those thousands of women?
>
> But I remembered him and the leather crop swinging from his belt. It was the first time since my release that I had been face to face with one of my captors and my blood seemed to freeze.
>
> 'You mentioned Ravensbrück in your talk,' he was saying. 'I was a guard in there.' No, he did not remember me.
>
> 'But since that time,' he went on, 'I have become a Christian. I know that God has forgiven me for the cruel things I did there, but I would like to hear it from your lips as well. *Fräulein*' – again the hand came out – 'will you forgive me?'

STOP

What would you do in that moment?

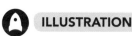

ILLUSTRATION

Corrie continues …

> And I stood there – I whose sins had every day to be forgiven – and could not. Betsie had died in that place – could he erase her slow terrible death simply for the asking?

> It could not have been many seconds that he stood there, hand held out, but to me it seemed hours as I wrestled with the most difficult thing I had ever had to do.

> For I had to do it – I knew that. The message that God forgives has a prior condition: that we forgive those who have injured us. 'If you do not forgive men their trespasses,' Jesus says, 'neither will your Father in heaven forgive your trespasses.'

God was asking Corrie to act out her faith and forgive, something easier said than done. She had seen with her own eyes people crippled with bitterness unable to rebuild their lives. She had also seen those who had forgiven their enemy rebuilding their lives despite the physical scars. In that moment as she wrestled with what to do, all the memories and familiar feelings must have come rushing back.

> 'Jesus, help me!' I prayed silently. 'I can lift my hand. I can do that much. You supply the feeling.' And so woodenly, mechanically, I thrust my hand into the one stretched out to me. And as I did, an incredible thing took place. The current started in my shoulder, raced down my arm, sprang into our joined hands. And then this healing warmth seemed to flood my whole being, bringing tears to my eyes. 'I forgive you, brother!' I cried. 'With all my heart!'[1]

---

1   'Guideposts Classics: Corrie ten Boom on Forgiveness' <https://www. guideposts.org/better-living/positive-living/guideposts-classics-corrie-ten-

I realise that Corrie's story mostly shows the forgiveness of her enemy, now a brother in Christ, but kindness, compassion and forgiveness are so closely interwoven that it's hard to separate one from the other. Her forgiveness, her shaking his hand, was a real act of kindness. She had to ask God to help her to do it, she struggled, but she did nonetheless show kindness to what was her enemy. It's fairly painless to be kind to someone we love, a friend or just a nice wee old granny needing her shopping carried up the stairs, but showing kindness to our enemies seems like an impossible task. And yet, what we see in Corrie is an example of the Lord doing the impossible by changing the hearts of His people. It may seem completely unrealistic, but with God all things are possible and thankfully, as we see in Corrie's story, we don't have to do it alone; God is with us, helping us.

Kindness is defined in God's character, displayed in person by Jesus through His life and work on earth and produced in the life of the believer by the Holy Spirit. Kindness must be displayed in the life of the believer.

> **STOP**
>
> How are you displaying kindness to those around you?

Alas, as with all things, we can take something that is beautiful, a characteristic of God, and warp and twist it. We can twist even kindness.

 'Be careful not to practice your righteousness in front of others to be seen by them. If you do, you will have no reward from your Father in heaven. So when you give to the needy, do not announce it with trumpets, as the hypocrites do in the synagogues and on the streets, to be honored by others. Truly I tell you, they have received their reward in full. But when you give to the needy, do not let your left hand know

boom-on-forgiveness> Accessed April 2019.

what your right hand is doing, so that your giving may be in secret. Then your Father, who sees what is done in secret, will reward you' (Matt. 6:1-4).

We see in Matthew a warning not to practise our righteousness for the wrong reasons, for selfish glory: being kind so that we can look good in front of other people, to get that pat on the back, be praised and noticed by them. That's not real kindness. That's about us and what we are getting out of it. 1 Corinthians 10:31 (ESV) says 'Whether you eat or drink, or whatever you do, do all to the glory of God'. So, whatever you do, when you are being kind, do it for God's glory and not your own glory.

STOP

How much of your kindness is done for personal glory? What are you getting out of it? What are you going to do about that?

JACKIE

If I'm being totally honest I like it when all the church folk think I'm being all helpful – it makes me feel good about myself. But I know I'm changing because now I would do it even if no one was looking.

There will be times when kindness is easy and we do it without even thinking, but God calls us to more than that. He calls us to the costly, difficult and seemingly impossible acts of kindness. Thankfully, He sends the Holy Spirit to produce this in our lives. So He not only asks us to display this, He also gives us all that we need to actually achieve it. If there is an act of kindness God is asking us to do that we simply find impossible, it's just too hard, then ask God for help. As we learned from Corrie's story, you can ask God to help us, change us, soften our hearts and give us the strength to do the impossible. He will help.

KEY POINT

We experience God's kindness through our salvation in Christ as He died a cruel death for us. This kindness should, by faith, be displayed in our lives as we look for ways to help people in need, no matter who they are and how much gratitude they show us.

MEMORY VERSE

'*But when the kindness of God our Savior and His love for mankind appeared, He saved us, not on the basis of deeds which we have done in righteousness, but according to His mercy, by the washing of regeneration and renewing by the Holy Spirit, whom He poured out upon us richly through Jesus Christ our Savior*' (Titus 3:4-6, NASB).

SUMMARY

Kindness is something we all understand but don't always show. When we do show kindness we expect people to be grateful. God's kindness to us is different; it isn't affected by how grateful we are. His kindness is defined by His character. This is something we see in the life of Jesus and experience for ourselves through salvation in Him. God even shows kindness to His enemies – something we wouldn't even consider. This is the type of kindness that must be displayed in our lives.

WHAT'S THE POINT?

Christians should grow in goodness.

6. WE ARE MADE FOR GOODNESS

 *'But the fruit of the Spirit is love, joy, peace, forbearance, kindness, **goodness**, faithfulness, gentleness and self-control. Against such things there is no law'* (Gal. 5:22-23).

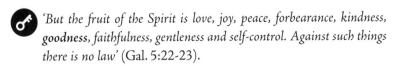

JACKIE

What is goodness? Is it just someone who is being good?

We use the word *good* all the time.

The movie was good

carrots are good for your eyes

I feel good about myself

she's good at football

he's a good cook

We say it loads, but what does it mean? And haven't we just talked about it in the last chapter? What's the difference between kindness and goodness? Aren't they just the same thing? If they are the same thing, then why does Paul list them as separate fruit in Galatians 5:22? There has to be some difference or he wouldn't have bothered. Or, is kindness just the acting out of being good?

Is there a difference between kindness and goodness? This was my question of the day yesterday; by this point my head was hurting so I decided to enlist some help. I asked a few people but to no avail: 'Oh, I'd have to think about that' was pretty much the standard answer from everyone – even the smart ones. Then our associate minister helpfully said to try googling Tim Keller as he has a definition of each fruit. Genius!

> *Agathosune* [the Greek word used in the New Testament; it was originally written in Greek] = goodness, integrity; being the same person in every situation, rather than a phony or a hypocrite. This is not the same as being always truthful but not always loving; getting things off your chest just to make yourself feel or look better.[1]

Having 'integrity' means being an honest person with strong moral principles who isn't two-faced or a fake. Now that's an old-fashioned word we don't hear used on a regular basis these days. Nowadays, it seems everyone squishes and smudges the truth to suit themselves. It's become so normal to lie that we may not even realise we are doing it, and actual honesty seems a distant memory. In fact, it seems that being honest sometimes sets us at a disadvantage. It can appear that every sphere of life is built on a lie in some way:

the super exciting Facebook status,

the truth that is stretched on our résumé or C.V. to get the job we're not quite qualified for,

ripping off the social by claiming benefits as a single parent when your man lives with you or claiming housing benefit for the flat you're sub-letting,

---

1   Tim Keller, *Galatians For You* (United Kingdom: The Good Book Company, 2013), p. 142. (Kindle Version)

claiming our phone was stolen when we sold it at cash convertors for £200,

even swearing on our granny's grave when she is alive and kicking.

To be honest the list is endless and that's the sad fact.

As I write this chapter one of the two top news stories talks about a human rights lawyer who brought false claims of torture and murder against British troops. He has admitted his misconduct to the tribunal, admitted to nine allegations of acting without integrity and recklessness – and yet he has denied dishonesty. How can that be possible? The other story is the Russian athlete doping scandal, suggesting a conspiracy that goes all the way to the top of the Russian government.

 James 5:12 (ESV) says *'But above all, my brothers, do not swear, either by heaven or by earth or by any other oath, but let your "yes" be yes and your "no" be no, so that you may not fall under condemnation.'*

Too often people pretend to have virtues, morals and principles that they don't actually possess. We fake it, but our actions deny our profession of faith. Even as Christians we aren't that honest. 'My word is my bond' is a motto that's been in use for centuries but, for us Christians, many of us simply can't be trusted to keep our word – our word is worthless, never mind our bond.

STOP

Are you living out your faith every day or faking it well? What does your life say about the goodness of the Lord?

 ### ILLUSTRATION

Jackie comes to see you one Monday morning after school drop-off. 'I'm freaking out. I got a letter from the social this morning and they want to make me go back to work. I'm not fit! They know I've got depression and a bad back. How can they expect me to work when I can't even get through the day? What if they sanction my money? What am I going to do?' Jackie shows you a letter which states she has a back-to-work assessment next week. She's a little more relaxed after you offer to come with her to the appointment.

The appointment date comes and as you pull up at Jackie's she gives you a wave from the window. As she leaves the house you notice she is not only looking very smart but is sporting a hospital-style crutch round her left arm and limping. She looks like she is having some real trouble walking. As she plonks herself in the front seat she looks at you and rolls her eyes. 'Look, before you even say anything to me, I've been talking to a few people and they told me I have to really emphasise my illness to get them to see it. It's not like I'm outright lying, I'm just exaggerating it a little so they can see how bad it really gets for me. I'm actually helping them assess me better. I knew you were gonna be all judgmental and I should have just got a taxi. It's easy for you – you've got a job. You don't know how hard it is for me.'

STOP

As a Christian what should Jackie be doing? How would you respond if it were you in the car?

 JACKIE

Jackie actually listened to what you had to say in the car that day and decided to be honest. 'I'm still a bit scared, though – trusting God is hard.' The crutch stayed with you in the car park when she went in for her assessment.

God's goodness shows us exactly who He is and what He is like; this should be displayed in our lives. His goodness is made up of righteousness, justice, mercy and forgiveness.

His works are good,

His commands are good,

His Word is good,

His gifts are good,

His ways are good,

He is upstanding and lacks nothing.

Everything He does is good.

 "Why do you ask me about what is good?" Jesus replied. "There is only One who is good. If you want to enter life, keep the commandments" (Matt. 19:17).

So, is it possible for us to display God's goodness in our lives when it is so exceptional and extraordinary? No matter how much we try, how much effort we put in, we simply can't be that good, can we? This time, surely, God is expecting the impossible of us.

 'But when the goodness and loving kindness of God our Savior appeared, he saved us, not because of works done by us in righteousness, but according to his own mercy, by the washing of regeneration and renewal of the Holy Spirit, whom he poured out on us richly through Jesus Christ our Savior, so that being justified by his grace we might become heirs according to the hope of eternal life.' (Titus 3:4-7, ESV)

STOP

Why is it possible for us to practise doing good in our lives?

The gospel makes it possible for us to display God's goodness in our lives as we express it through our faith in action. Thankfully, we don't have to do that in our own strength – let's face it, we'd be useless anyway. Most of us have the willpower of a gnat. Ephesians 2:8-9 tells us that God's the one who does this work in our lives, so we can't boast about our own strength of will or ability. Paul writes, 'For it is by grace you have been saved, through faith – and this is not from yourselves, it is the gift of God – not by works, so that no one can boast. For we are God's handiwork, created in Christ Jesus to do good works, which God prepared in advance for us to do.'

God's the one who transforms us and makes this possible. That doesn't mean we just sit back, feet up, and do nothing. Heart change really comes from God. He is the one who transforms us, but He expects us to put that change into practice.

 'Finally, brothers and sisters, whatever is true, whatever is noble, whatever is right, whatever is pure, whatever is lovely, whatever is admirable – if anything is excellent or praiseworthy – think about such things. Whatever you have learned or received or heard from me, or seen in me – **put it into practice.** *And the God of peace will be with you'* (Phil. 4:8-9).

In his book *The Fruitful Life* the author Jerry Bridges says,

> **Remember that most opportunities for doing good come across the ordinary path of our day. Don't look for the spectacular; few people ever have the opportunity to pull a victim from the wreckage of a flaming automobile. All of us have opportunity to administer the kind or encouraging word – to do a little, perhaps unseen, deed that makes life more pleasant for someone else.[2]**

---

2   Jerry Bridges, *The Fruitful Life* (Colorado Springs, CO: NavPress, 2006), p. 127. (Kindle Version)

Jerry Bridges reminds us that it's not just in the extraordinary or even special moments of life that we need to show God's goodness, but in the everyday, humdrum, boring, ordinary moments. The truth is we probably find it easier to remember to engage our brain and think about practising goodness when we are at church, but at home it may be different. In those little everyday moments when we are just strolling through life with our family, our brains are often in neutral; we forget and all thoughts of goodness go out the window.

But the little things matter.

STOP

Who are you struggling to show goodness to and why?

It's in these moments, when we are struggling for whatever reason to practise God's goodness, that we need to pause and have a wee reality check. We forget far too easily who we are and what we have done. God knows our deepest darkest thoughts; He knows the real us, even the bits we can't admit to ourselves, and yet, still He shows us His goodness through the gospel. That's an amazing gift – that's grace, and because of that we must make every effort to practise that goodness, even to those we are struggling to love.

KEY POINT

Everything God does is good. God's goodness is made up of His righteousness, justice, mercy and forgiveness. His works are good, His commands are good, His Word is good, His gifts are good, His ways are good – He is upstanding and lacks nothing.

 ### MEMORY VERSE

'Surely goodness and mercy shall follow me all the days of my life, and I shall dwell in the house of the LORD forever.' (Ps. 23:6, ESV)

SUMMARY

Even though we use the word *good* all the time we struggle to really pin down what it means. As Christians we are called to grow in goodness which means live with integrity, being honest, not being two-faced or being a phoney. Everything God does is good. His goodness shows exactly who He is and what He is like – righteous, just, merciful and forgiving. This is the goodness that should be displayed in our lives.

WHAT'S THE POINT?

Christians should grow in faithfulness.

7. LOVE MAKES FAITHFULNESS EASY, RIGHT?

'*But the fruit of the Spirit is love, joy, peace, forbearance, kindness, goodness, **faithfulness**, gentleness and self-control. Against such things there is no law*' (Gal. 5:22-23).

In December 2015 Karam and Katari Chand from Bradford celebrated their 90th wedding anniversary. They were officially the world's longest married couple until Karam died the following year. How amazing is that? They were faithful to one another for ninety years – that's nearly a century. This kind of fidelity, loyalty and faithfulness is rare nowadays. Every day there are stories splashed all over the tabloids and magazines with sensational headlines of cheaters caught red-handed. We all know tales of families that have being torn apart and destroyed by unfaithfulness. This might make for sensational reading in the papers, but the truth behind these headlines will no doubt be devastatingly painful. Sadly, divorce rates are climbing through the roof as promises to remain true made on wedding days become a long-forgotten memory. Faithfulness seems like an optional extra when people are on their second or third marriage.

The Bible calls us as Christians to grow in faithfulness. So what does faithfulness actually mean? Faithfulness means to be completely reliable and true to our word. Most of us have a best friend, someone who has been with you through thick and thin. You know they are completely loyal and keep their word. You can and have trusted them with your deepest darkest secret, and you're absolutely certain they haven't breathed a single word to anyone. In fact, we know that they would keep their word even if it were costly to them because they have done it in the past. They're a proper diamond! This is the faithfulness I'm talking about, faithfulness that is motivated by our affections and is 100 per cent loyal in heart and mind.

This is what we are called to in our relationship with God. We are called to be 100 per cent faithful to Him as He is faithful to us.

'*Know therefore that the Lord your God is God; he is the faithful God, keeping his covenant of love to a thousand generations of those who love him and keep his commandments*' (Deut. 7:9).

God is completely and utterly faithful. He is always reliable, totally trustworthy, never changes, absolutely true to His word, and completely loyal. You see, it is in God's very nature to be faithful – it's who He is.

Deuteronomy 32:4 says, '*The Rock, his work is perfect, for all his ways are justice. A God of faithfulness and without iniquity, just and upright is he.*' (esv)

Out of God's faithfulness to Himself, God is faithful to His people. Moses says in Deuteronomy 7:9 (esv) that God '**keeps covenant and steadfast love with those who love him.**' This covenant is a binding agreement between two people, like a contract but weightier. It's also more personal, like you would find in marriage vows. But there is one major difference when God makes a covenant promise. Unlike the contract or marriage vows, this covenant is an agreement made between two *unequal* parties. After all, He is GOD. When God makes a covenant He sets the agenda, He makes the rules, it's non-negotiable, and unlike us He always keeps His promise. His Word is as solid as it comes.

The same can't be said for us, as I've no doubt we will all be able to testify. It can be pretty common to break or go back on a promise. To be honest, we behave sometimes like it's no big deal. We make promises all the time. We promise to visit our granny, we promise to take the kids out, we promise to do the dishes and we promise ourselves that this is the last cigarette.

We often break promises.

STOP

When was the last time you promised to do something? Did you do it?

When God makes a covenant with His people He always keeps it. He is completely dependable and keeps His Word.

God doesn't change His mind and never breaks a promise.

JACKIE

How can I trust that's true?

'God is not man, that he should lie, or a son of man, that he should change his mind. Has he said, and will he not do it? Or has he spoken, and will he not fulfil it?' (Num. 23:19, ESV)

God made a covenant with Abraham (Gen. 12), promising that He would make his seed into a great nation and bless them, promising to give them their own land for a home. God kept that promise. But Abraham must have wondered if God was going to be faithful, because it took decades for God to make good on His Word. Abraham didn't have his son Isaac until he was 100 years old. One kid's not a nation, though, is it? If we draw the family tree from Isaac, adding his children and then his grandchildren, eventually if we keep going you will find this little family became the nation of Israel. God was absolutely faithful to His promise to Abraham. Time and time again through the Bible we see God being faithful to His promise.

'God spoke to Moses and said to him, "I am the LORD. I appeared to Abraham, to Isaac, and to Jacob, as God Almighty, but by my name the LORD I did not make myself known to them. I also established my covenant with them to give them the land of Canaan, the land in which they lived as sojourners. Moreover, I have heard the groaning of the people of Israel whom the Egyptians hold as slaves, and I have remembered my covenant. Say therefore to the people of Israel: I am the LORD, and I will bring you out from under the burdens of the Egyptians, and I will deliver you from slavery to them, and I will redeem you with an outstretched arm and with great acts of judgement."' (Exod. 6:2-6, ESV)

Generations after their ancestors Abraham and Isaac, Israel must have thought God was unfaithful. They were suffering, held captive as slaves in Egypt. They must have asked themselves if God had broken His Word to bless them and give them a home. But as we see from Exodus 6:2-6, God made a promise and He is going to keep it.

You might be thinking, 'OK, Sharon, nice history lesson and much shorter than the *Prince of Egypt* version, but what's that got to do with me today?' It has loads to do with us today, because as Christians we are now part of the same covenant promise God made to Abraham, through the blood of Jesus. We are His people. He's rescued us and promised us a Christian homeland, heaven! God always keeps His promises.

He will be faithful to us, and thankfully His faithfulness isn't dependent on us; He is faithful despite our

sin,

weaknesses

and failures.

Although we are unfaithful to Him, He remains faithful to us.

That's not an excuse to whoop it up and live however we want, embracing every sin we can think of! But it's a promise that even if we fail and let Him down, He will be true and faithful concerning His promises to us. He doesn't change. He is dependable. We can trust in Him. He is faithful. So I'm going to bang that same drum, asking how this applies to our lives. God is **faithful** to His people and we must display His faithfulness in our lives. We need to understand that when we became Christians, we entered into one of these covenants with God that we talked about earlier. We are in a relationship with Him and called as His children to be faithful and true to Him.

We are to be a faithful people.

STOP

What do you think that looks like?

Being true and faithful to God means we need to put Him first. That's easy to say but hard to do. We chase after things, making them more important to us than God. The Bible calls these idols. We say we are 100 per cent committed to God and then when the next good-looking guy, chance to get some extra cash, or opportunity to have some fun or pleasure comes along, we put God aside. We tell ourselves it's just for a moment and we lie to ourselves and ultimately forsake Him. The Bible uses words we might think harsh, but it calls us prostitutes, saying we go whoring after other things.

We cheat on God left, right and centre.

Strong words but the harsh reality!

JACKIE

After Frank left her, Jackie's mum was helpful but it wasn't really the same; life was tough being a single mum. Jackie really struggled, but no matter how much she wanted to make their relationship work, he refused – he just couldn't forgive her. Things had been slowly falling apart before the court case, but now she's a Christian he's become even more hostile. She knows what she did was wrong, but nothing she says or does seems to fix it. She's said sorry a million times but he'll never forgive her … the truth was hard for her to face. In the end she simply had no choice but to accept the reality. But she was lonely and she missed him.

ILLUSTRATION

Jackie was spending more and more time on social media. She was back in touch with an old school pal who, on finding out Jackie was single again, suggested she try online dating. Jackie was hesitant at first and did question whether, as a Christian, this was right. 'What are the rules now?' She spent a while weighing it up in her mind – well, five minutes to be honest. Would God be happy with this?

The more Jackie thought about it the more she started to tell herself, 'What have I got to lose?' So she signed up. At first it was just the odd message to a guy. She hadn't really spent much time on her profile, but the more she got chatting to blokes by private message, the more time she was spending online instead of with her kids. Soon it became the first thing she did in the morning, every spare second she got, and last thing at night. Things were getting so bad that Jackie beefed up her phone package so she could check her messages all the time. Jackie hadn't yet agreed to go on a date, she just liked the chat. 'Good to have the male side of the conversation,' she told herself. If she was being honest she enjoyed flirting. The conversations had occasionally become a bit sexual, with suggestive comments. Jackie didn't really see this as an issue; it wasn't like she was actually having sex, after all. She said to herself, 'It's just make-believe.' When the girls from church tried to meet up with her, she was far too busy. She'd even missed the odd Sunday. She'd been up late into the night messaging and was just too tired to get up.

STOP

Who or what has become more important to Jackie than God?

We don't wake up one morning ten miles from God, and drifting away doesn't happen overnight. As we read in Jackie's story, the drift happened a little bit at a time. She gave over her affection to something and someone else. Where once God was important to her, the pleasure of being loved by a guy took over – it became what drove her actions. We are called to be faithful in our affections towards God and love Him first. We shouldn't chase after idols but be wholly obedient to God – 100 percent commitment is what He wants.

JACKIE

After being really challenged by a sermon one day, Jackie realised she'd been a complete idiot, and when it was all quiet she prayed and asked God to forgive her. When she was talking it through with her friend Miriam later, she admitted how much she was really missing Frank and how lonely she was. 'I know God's more important to me than any man. I just find it hard to remember that.'

STOP

Who or what has become more important to you than God? Are you handing over your affection to something or someone else?

Jesus says we are to love God with all our hearts, all our minds and all our strength (Mark 12:30). That's everything we've got. God is not just to be a little bit on the side, something we pick up on a Sunday morning and Wednesday evening, like a part-time relationship. No, He wants the whole of your life.

'And you shall love the Lord your God with all your heart and with all your soul and with all your mind and with all your strength' (Mark 12:30, ESV).

Not only are we to be faithful to God, but also faithful to **one another**. We ought to be true to our word even when it costs us big time and hurts. In the big things and the small things. Luke 16:10 (ESV) says: **'One who is faithful in a very little is also faithful in much, and one who is dishonest in a very little is also dishonest in much.'**

Faithfulness is born in the small things of life as we keep plodding on; it's what we do when no one is looking.

It's how we manage the small amounts of money we've got, how, no matter what little cash there is, we still give to God's work, how we tell the truth even in the seemingly incidental things of life, how we squelch that little unhelpful thought before it becomes massive.... God honours this kind of faithfulness.

'And if you faithfully obey the voice of the LORD your God, being careful to do all his commandments that I command you today, the LORD your God will set you high above all the nations of the earth' (Deut. 28:1, ESV).

STOP

What do you think is going on when you don't *feel* the blessings of the Lord in your life?

When we disobey and are unfaithful there are consequences – we have to pay the piper, as my mum would say. We don't like to think of consequences in the heat of the moment, when our minds are weighing up wisdom versus folly, or when we want to chase after sinful things.

But we can't expect to move forward in our Christian lives while we are being disobedient to God.

It just doesn't work like that.

Think about it: if a guy cheated on his wife again and again, would we really expect them to have a healthy relationship? Do we think she would trust him? Would they be communicating well? Not a chance! It's exactly the same in our relationship with God. **When we are in persistent sin and disobedience, our relationships with God can't be healthy, we won't be trusted, our communication will be down the pan.** We might be looking at our lives thinking we should be further on in our Christian walk. Maybe, even though we've been persistently praying, we don't feel close to God. The reason may be that we're unfaithful. We need to stop running after other things.

 'If we confess our sins, he is faithful and just to forgive us our sins and to cleanse us from all unrighteousness' (1 John 1:9, ESV).

KEY POINT

We are unfaithful to God when we chase and lust after the desires of our hearts. We must repent, confess and return in faithfulness to God.

 ### MEMORY VERSE

'Let us hold fast the confession of our hope without wavering, for he who promised is faithful' (Heb. 10:23, ESV).

We are an unfaithful people but Christ will hold us fast. And so let us in response faithfully worship Him with all that we have! Let us hold fast our confession. Let us adore Him. Let us love Him more than anything else. Let us worship Him with all that we have – because He is worthy!

 SUMMARY

Many of us simply wouldn't think of being unfaithful to someone we loved yet we are unfaithful to God all too often. God is completely and utterly faithful. He is always reliable, totally trustworthy, never changes, absolutely true to His Word, and unflinchingly loyal to His people. In our weakness, on account of His faithfulness, Christ forgives us. What an encouragement. He will hold us fast until the end because He is faithful. He cannot deny Himself (2 Tim. 2:13).

WHAT'S THE POINT?

Christians should grow in gentleness.

8. BEING GENTLE MEANS WE'RE JUST WEAK, RIGHT?

*'But the fruit of the Spirit is love, joy, peace, forbearance, kindness, goodness, faithfulness, **gentleness** and self-control. Against such things there is no law'* (Gal. 5:22-23).

When I was a young Christian I totally misunderstood the meaning of gentleness. For us girlies I thought it meant we had to be all mousey and quiet, you know what I mean? The nice and quiet type – soft! For the blokes I thought gentleness meant they were a pushover who never stood up to anyone and never rocked the boat. Vanilla, I called it – weak, drab and boring.

> **STOP**
>
> What's the first word that pops into your head when you're asked what gentleness means?

'Come to me, all you who are weary and burdened, and I will give you rest. Take my yoke upon you and learn from me, for I am gentle and humble in heart, and you will find rest for your souls. For my yoke is easy and my burden is light' (Matt. 11:28-30).

> **STOP**
>
> How is Jesus described in Matthew?

We know there is no way that Jesus, who is God, can be described as weak – in the sense I have described it above. It simply isn't true and He never had an issue standing up to anyone. Time and time again when He needed to, He stood up to the religious leaders and called them out, straight to their faces. Like in Matthew 23:13 when He says 'But, woe to you scribes and Pharisees, hypocrites! For you lock people out of the kingdom of heaven.' This is definitely not a picture of a pushover! So, if your description of gentleness is very similar to my young Christian version, you need to rethink what it means and the impact that has on your life.

Gentleness is far more about strength under control, like reining yourself in for the other person's benefit.

 ILLUSTRATION

Jackie's pal Adele had been going to the gym for a couple of years. One of her favourite classes was Boxing Circuits. The class went through various stations, each one a different task like rope work or core strength, but her absolute favourite was when she got the gloves on and could spar with a partner. Even though she had a short reach she could pack a punch and was well renowned for not holding back. She rattled a few heads.

This week Adele brought Jackie with her. Jackie had decided she had let herself go, and let's face it, if anyone was ever going to look twice at her, she needed to get her act together and do something about it. Jackie was a bit nervous as she hadn't really done a class before, but Adele would keep her straight.

The two paired as they went round the circuits. When they came to the sparring station Jackie said, 'Remember, I'm a newbie – go easy on me.' So for once Adele pulled her punches, taking it easy and giving Jackie the opportunity to work on technique.

Let's think about this illustration. Jackie is asking Adele to 'go easy' – to be gentle. She wasn't saying Adele was a weakling, but was asking her to hold back her strength for her sake. Adele was more than capable of letting it fly, she was more than able to fight, but held back her strength for Jackie's benefit.

It's easy for a strong character to use their strength to get what they want, to over-rule and overshadow another, but that's not true strength, is it? That's just being overbearing, harsh, pushy, maybe even a bit of a bully. There's a temptation for those who are strong to write it off and excuse their behaviour, simply saying 'it's just who I am'. But, as we have been finding out throughout this book, that's a feeble excuse that doesn't have any legs. It's simply not good enough to brush it aside like it's not important. If someone is scared, apprehensive or afraid to share their opinion in front of you, then there is something wrong.

This is why I've been avoiding writing this chapter. As a strong and frankly formidable personality I have spent much time reflecting on the fruit of *Gentleness*. Jerry Bridges, in his book *The Fruitful Life*, suggests that it's not a characteristic like love or patience that we pray for, but that wouldn't be true of me. In fact, I think that of all the fruit we have discussed so far, I have prayed for gentleness more than any of the others. I am well aware of who I am and my strengths and weaknesses.

When I was a young Christian I thought I had to conform and be like those around me. I reined in who I was so much that *I* became vanilla, a former shadow of myself. It grieved me – it was crushingly painful. I was a round peg trying to fit into a square hole. It's not helpful thinking, and if you're reading this thinking 'Man, that's exactly how I feel. I'm sick of pretending I am someone I'm not,' then stop it.

It's not helpful or honest.

We have been fearfully and wonderfully made by God for His purpose.

He knows what He is doing.

'But by the grace of God I am what I am, and his grace to me was not without effect. No, I worked harder than all of them – yet not I, but the grace of God that was with me' (1 Cor. 15:10).

'I praise you because I am fearfully and wonderfully made; your works are wonderful; I know that full well' (Ps. 139:14).

I particularly love what Paul emphasises about his character in 1 Corinthians 15:10: 'I am what I am, and his grace to me was not without effect.' It reminds us that, no matter what, God's grace impacts us, so we can't excuse our sinful behaviours just because we are a particular personality type. Consistently throughout the New Testament we find verse after verse talking about gentleness and meekness, stressing that it is something we should seek.

Galatians 5 is clear: gentleness is a characteristic of God and we should display that in our lives – all of us.

Not just the annoying, the angry, the feisty, the loud, the passionate, the outspoken, the harsh, the blunt, the intimidating, the formidable, but ALL of us. This isn't a fruit for just one type of Christian, but for all Christians.

STOP

Who do you find it most hard to be gentle towards – why?

 ILLUSTRATION

Standing outside Mary's funeral, Nan and Jackie were chatting. 'She got a good send-off today,' said Jackie. Nan looked at her and paused for a second before she launched: 'That minister they had leading the service was a bit weird, don't you think; and the flowers – what were they thinking? It's not necessary to have all those flowers; they just get wasted. I don't know what they were thinking – it's not like Mary actually gets to see them. They must have spent a fortune. What a complete waste of money. What is it they say when someone is trying to overcompensate for something, that's what it is – they should have paid more attention to her when she was alive ...' Before Nan had much more chance to continue, Jackie shushed her. 'Nan! People will hear. You're not exactly being quiet, are you?' Nan, annoyed at being stopped halfway through a rant, scowled. 'I'm just telling it like it is. It's the truth!'

Nan might have hit the nail on the head or she might be an old bat who needs to repent and keep her opinions to herself. Truth or not, she is speaking without thought for her hearer. She's not exactly being the poster child for gentleness. Gentle Christians will not only rein themselves in for others' benefit but will be respectful of other people's opinions and feelings. They will be considerate, engaging their brain before they talk, thinking not only about the truthfulness of their words but how they are said. Gentle Christians speak truth but not without consideration of how it's heard and received. They don't feel the need to degrade, humiliate or gossip about another Christian who has fallen into sin; instead they'd be sad, grieving for them and praying for their repentance (see Gal. 6:1).

'Therefore, as God's chosen people, holy and dearly loved, clothe yourselves with compassion, kindness, humility, gentleness and patience' (Col. 3:12).

We are God's people, His representatives, and we are to clothe ourselves and put on gentleness. As with all these chapters, we need to have an honest look at ourselves in how we speak and deal with people. It's not enough for us just to recognise and admit it – we need to repent and turn to God for help. We must cultivate gentleness; we need to ask the Lord for help to develop in us a gentle spirit.

STOP

On a scale of 0 – 10 how would you rate yourself?

a. I can usually tell when someone isn't their usual self

b. I can be sensitive to other people's feelings

c. I intimidate and scare people

d. I am outspokenly critical of other people

e. I pride myself on always telling it as it is – no matter who is listening

f. I speak to all people with respect

g. I only speak respectfully to those that have earned it

h. I am blunt and abrupt

i. I listen to reason

j. I always share my point of view and never back down

k. I can be resentful of people who oppose me

STOP

What aspects of gentleness would you like to develop in yourself?

KEY POINT

Gentleness is a quality that means I am constantly thinking, 'How can I use my strength and abilities to serve others?'

 ## MEMORY VERSE

'But in your hearts revere Christ as Lord. Always be prepared to give an answer to everyone who asks you to give the reason for the hope that you have. But do this with gentleness and respect' (1 Pet. 3:15).

SUMMARY

Our twisted minds, can think gentleness is just another word for weakness. Gentleness is far more about strength which is under control, like reining ourselves in for the other person's benefit or being considerate and respectful about what we say as well as how it's heard. Our all-powerful God isn't pushy, brash or overbearing. He is gentle to us and we must imitate His gentleness in the way we care for each other.

WHAT'S THE POINT?

Christians should grow in self-control.

9. DOING WHAT'S NEEDED EVEN WHEN YOU DON'T WANT TO: SELF-CONTROL

 *'But the fruit of the Spirit is love, joy, peace, forbearance, kindness, goodness, faithfulness, gentleness and **self-control**. Against such things there is no law'* (Gal. 5:22-23).

The irony of eating from a tub of Ben & Jerry's whilst writing a chapter on self-control is not lost on me at all. As I write this it's just two weeks until Christmas and I've already had one Christmas dinner. Next week I will have three. We tell ourselves the lie that in January we will be extra good, and so we give ourselves permission to enjoy all the festive indulgences and tasty bites. Not thinking about the scales, we sit on the sofa with a tin of chocolates and watch *The Sound of Music* for the umpteenth time, stuffing our face without restraint. 'Just one more' rules, even though we know that 'just one more' feeds the desire to have yet another.

But Christmas isn't the only time we lack self-control. We just need to watch a kid in a sweet or toy shop as they demand everything in sight, followed by a massive tantrum when they are told no. Imagine if there were no consequences and no 'NO' word, free rein to do whatever and consume whatever we fancy without limits. For about a millisecond it sounds like it could be a good plan – then we start to think about it. A kid could eat all the sweets he likes, an alcoholic could drink as much as he wants, the drug addict could simply keep consuming his passion, the girl with the credit card buys everything in sight, someone spends all their time watching porn as their taste gets darker and darker. A world without restraint would be chaos, everyone doing as they please, no matter the cost.

 'I denied myself nothing my eyes desired; I refused my heart no pleasure. My heart took delight in all my labor, and this was the reward for all my toil' (Eccles. 2:10).

 'Everyone did what was right in his own eyes' (Judg. 21:25, ESV).

> **STOP**
>
> Think about Ephesians 4:19. What does it say the cost is for living a life without control? What do you think would be the pros and cons for living a life without restraint?

Whether it's the extra kilos we've put on, the tooth decay, or, at the extreme end of the spectrum, drug addiction or cirrhosis of the liver, a lack of self-control always has a cost. Ed Welch in an article about self-control makes an interesting point when he says, 'It is true that many addicts, when their private addictions are exposed, experience pain, but the pain is more often the result of being caught than a distaste for the actual addictive substances.'[1] Living without constraint comes at a price whether we admit it to ourselves or not. But as Ed Welch points out, those who are only worried about the immediate pain that comes from being caught and busted are pretty oblivious to the real cost of their actions – a cost that may be paid for by their families and not them. The drug-addict mum is not likely to admit to herself that she loves her drugs more than her kids, but when they go to get food and the cupboards are empty, the truth is evident. Oh, she may feel

---

1   Ed Welch, 'Self-Control: The Battle Against "One More"', *The Journal of Biblical Counseling*, Volume 19, Number 2 (Winter 2001), p. 25.

bad, maybe even devastated that she's let them down *again*, but not enough to give up her first love – drugs. 'The truth, however, is that, no matter how tragic the consequences of the sin, there is some pleasure in it.'[2]

We almost always underestimate sin and the pull it has on us. Sin is attractive and pleasurable; well, at least it is in the beginning. Hebrews 11:25 says the pleasures of sin are fleeting.

It may be pleasurable but the pleasure is temporary.

We lie to ourselves that after just one more time we will be satisfied. In reality all that happens is that we feed the desire for 'yet another'. Sin never satisfies, it always leaves us wanting more. Ephesians 4:19 says, 'Having lost all sensitivity, they have given themselves over to sensuality so as to indulge in every kind of impurity, and they are full of greed.'

We are never satisfied.

Ultimately what we are saying is that God isn't enough for us.

> **STOP**
>
> Is there something in your life you think might have become an idol? Is something more important to you than God?

Self-Control means living within God's boundaries that He has put in place for our good, our protection, our well-being and His glory.

 ILLUSTRATION

Jackie takes wee Frankie to visit her old Aunty Mona one day. Jackie loves her Aunty Mona even if she's still living in the dark ages – she still has the old-fashioned coal fire and back boiler in

---

2   Ibid.

her front room. Picture the scene. Wee Frankie loves the look of the fire. Since the first time he saw it he's been mesmerised by the dancing flames. He knows not to touch it, but today he couldn't resist. Slowly he reaches out his chubby wee toddler hand to touch. 'Frankie, NO, burny, burny!' Jackie says. Wee Frankie withdraws his hand quickly, sad that he can't play with the glowing fire. Wee Frankie waits as long as he can stand. Fascinated by the flames, he tries again. 'Frankie, I said NO!' Jackie says, much firmer this time. We all know where this is going. It's the simplest of illustrations but effective. Wee Frankie is completely aware he isn't allowed to touch the fire. Unaware the boundaries are there for his protection and safety, he simply, in his defiant toddler's mind, thinks mummy's being mean, with-holding a new delight. It's only when the inevitable happens and his fingers are burnt that he learns the lesson to live within the boundaries Jackie sets.

 JACKIE

I'm glad Mona was there to sort his fingers. I went to pieces. Frank wasn't well pleased at all that the little man had hurt himself either, but I'm learning not to respond to his digs all the time. I don't think Frank knows what to do with me now I'm not in his face screaming all the time.

Do you remember being a kid and seeing builders lay fresh cement? It was beautifully smooth and although you knew you shouldn't, you just had to squish your handprint in, leaving it there for posterity. Or when you're in the park and the sign says NO WALKING ON THE GRASS, but it's the shortest route and everyone else does it.

If there is a line drawn in the sand, the temptation for us all is to walk over it.

We resist boundaries and think anything resembling a rule is just a suggestion.

We see boundaries as some sort of evil punishment or a with-holding of our rights, and in some way, shape or form we persuade ourselves that they are an infringement of our personal freedom. Even when we know it's for our protection and good the temptation is there to please ourselves. Basically, **boundaries usually get in the way of us getting something we want,** think we need and therefore must have, which means they *must* be bad.

 '*Like a city whose walls are broken through is a person who lacks self-control*' (Prov. 25:28).

A city wall protects the people living inside, keeping them safe and secure. But a crumbling wall is as much use as a chocolate fireguard.

It's the same with self-control.

It's for our benefit and protection.

It may mean that we have to think before we act, resist temptation, and engage our brains, but we need it. The evil one will lie to us, spinning a thread of deceit. He will try to persuade us that the sin we are about to indulge in isn't really that bad, can easily be justified and isn't our fault. He will attempt to bring doubt into our minds, implying that God doesn't have our best interests at heart and that He doesn't know what's best for us. He will grab every single opportunity to sidetrack us into worshipping the creation instead of the Creator. The trouble is we can be our own worst enemy! We see this clearly in the book of James when he says:

 '*When tempted, no one should say, "God is tempting me." For God cannot be tempted by evil, nor does he tempt anyone; but each person is tempted when they are dragged away by their own evil desire and*

enticed. Then, after desire has conceived, it gives birth to sin; and sin, when it is full-grown, gives birth to death' (James 1:13-15).

James doesn't pull his punches when he says it is our own evil desires that conceive and give birth to sin. When we do not practise restraint or self-control, indulging in the lust of our hearts, whatever that may be, we sell out and give ourselves wholeheartedly to something other than God. We love something more than God and we worship it and not Him. And as you see, the consequences are grave.

Jerry Bridges was surely right when he said, 'External temptations would not be nearly so dangerous were it not for the fact they find an ally of desire right within our own breast.'[3]

STOP

What do you think Jerry Bridges is saying and how do you see that manifest itself in your life?

 'Therefore, my beloved, flee from idolatry' (1 Cor. 10:14, ᴇsᴠ).

 'Flee from sexual immorality. Every other sin a person commits is outside the body, but the sexually immoral person sins against his own body' (1 Cor. 6:18, ᴇsᴠ).

The Bible is clear: idols are dangerous and we need to FLEE from them – we need to bolt! The trouble is, we flee what we should pursue and pursue what we should flee. Luke is very clear in Luke 9:23: 'Then he [Jesus] said to them all: "Whoever wants to be my disciple must deny themselves and take up their cross daily and follow me."'

If we are followers of Christ – His disciples – then we must deny ourselves and be obedient. I realise it's not as easy as it sounds. If

---

3   Jerry Bridges, *The Fruitful Life*, p. 154. (Kindle Version)

it were, then the 'Just Say No' anti-drug campaign of the 80s in Britain would have been a huge success and we wouldn't have had to listen to the dreadful song for aeons. If it were really that simple, then we would all be able to easily walk away from temptation. We wouldn't look at the cream cake twice,

we'd choose food over drugs any day of the week,

we'd resist the temptation to gossip,

avoid *'accidentally on purpose'* turning on the adult channel,

and every word that came out of our mouths would be for building each other up.

We need help. We need help to fight the battle against the old self and rely totally on Christ.

STOP

So how do we do it? How do we practise self-control?

Recently I was listening to a sermon on this subject by a guy called Alistair Begg and he puts it something like this: 'Freedom isn't the liberty to do what we like but the willingness to do what is right.'[4] Thankfully, we aren't on our own in this.

God, through His Holy Spirit, puts the desire in our hearts.

Self-control is possible because of the grace given us in Jesus Christ and we need to rely on Him.

---

4   Alistair Begg, 'The Fruit of the Spirit' series, No 9: Self-Control. <https://www.truthforlife.org/resources/series/fruit-of-the-spirit/> Accessed April 2019.

We need God's grace. Ed Welch says, 'Only the grace of God takes self-control out of the realm of hopeless self-reformation into that of great confidence that we can be transformed people.'[5]

 JACKIE

Is the battle for self-control different for us all?

We all struggle and flourish in different areas and we all have different strengths and weaknesses. Some of us go through life simply trading one idol for another, never fully acknowledging the truth or recognising our need to depend on Christ. We need to be honest with ourselves and God. Proverbs 27:12 says, 'The prudent see danger and take refuge, but the simple keep going and pay the penalty.' We know we need to be honest and recognise the dangers in ourselves, assessing our spiritual need, and take refuge in Christ. We need to own it by taking responsibility and going before a merciful God in repentance and prayer, surrendering to the authority He has in our lives and living obediently within His boundaries.

STOP

What sinful thoughts have hounded you this week? (Lust, resentment, anger, selfishness, self-pity etc.)

The battle for self-control is fought primarily in our minds.

What starts as a tiny thought can quickly, without check, snowball into sin. It's like our brains are fine-tuned to the temptation that will hit our sin buttons the hardest. We need to pray for the strength to 'take captive every thought to make it obedient to Christ' (2 Cor. 10:5) and curb the desire whilst it's a wee ember and not fuel it into a burning flame. **If you're struggling with self-control, speak to a mature believer and ask them to pray for**

5   Ed Welch, 'Self-Control: The Battle Against "One More"', p. 30.

you and keep you accountable. They will help you think through your thought patterns and actions, not as recrimination but to help you be ready for the next battle – it's coming. Forewarned is forearmed, and prior knowledge of possible dangers or problems gives you a tactical advantage. It helps us to prepare, stand firm and be ready to flee at the first hint of temptation. This is what self-control looks like.

KEY POINT

Self-control means that we live within God's boundaries and obediently submit to Christ's control.

 'Above all else guard your heart, for everything you do flows from it' (Prov. 4:23).

 ### JACKIE

> When I think of being self-controlled I know it's not natural. My go-to is to instinctively respond and lash out with some smart, hurtful comment. I'm confessing and praying Jesus changes me because I can't do it on my own – it's too hard. But I know I'm not the same person I was the day I became a Christian. I am growing slowly and changing and it's freaking everyone out, especially Frank and the kids. I know they see the difference and can't explain it. I know they are secretly interested and paying attention. They've even asked a question or two.

Like Jackie, as a Christian, you need to not only talk the talk, but walk the walk with the Lord's help. We need to do more than confess Christ with our words; we should be changed by Him. He should be evident in our lives, and if He is we will see the Fruit of the Spirit. Growth and change may be slow, but as a Christian you should be becoming more like Christ every day. If there is no evidence of God in your life, then I would seriously question your salvation.

STOP

Am I growing in the fruit of the Spirit?

'I love those who love me, and those who seek me find me. With me are riches and honor, enduring wealth and prosperity. My fruit is better than fine gold; what I yield surpasses choice silver. I walk in the way of righteousness, along the paths of justice, bestowing a rich inheritance on those who love me and making their treasuries full' (Prov. 8:17-21).

When you struggle, when you fail, when you fall … run to God. Repent, cling to Him and keep on keeping on.

KEY POINT

Self-control means we must live within God's boundaries. Boundaries that He has put in place for our good, our protection, our well-being and His glory.

MEMORY VERSE

'But the fruit of the Spirit is love, joy, peace, forbearance, kindness, goodness, faithfulness, gentleness and self-control. Against such things there is no law' (Gal. 5:22-23).

SUMMARY

We underestimate sin and the pull it has on us. Sin is attractive and pleasurable (in the beginning) but such pleasure never lasts. We lie to ourselves saying 'just one more time and we will be satisfied'. All that happens is that we feed the desire and then want more. Sin never satisfies, it always leaves us wanting more. When we sin we are really saying that God isn't enough for us. As Christians we must live within the boundaries God has given us. They are there for our good, protection, well-being and His glory.

CONCLUSION

When we become a Christian we really do change and grow as we become more like Jesus. It's not like we become some sort of brainwashed robot who has suddenly turned into a shadow of our former self – you know, the vanilla bland version. But, as we grow to know Jesus more, as the Holy Spirit works in our lives and God challenges our dodgy thinking and behaviour, we change and grow.

If we aren't changing and growing, even at a snail's pace, then something is hinky. I'd go so far as to question whether or not the person has truly been saved – 'real Christian or a fake Christian?' As Christians we should be continually growing more and more like Christ. It's the same for Jackie. She might be able to fake it for five minutes but day in day out, from year to year, through the good times and the bad, as she continues to grow, the evidence of God's work in her life will be hard for anyone to deny. Even for Frank. So, if the evidence is in plain sight what does it say about us:

'real Christian or a fake Christian?'

IX 9Marks

This series of short workbooks, from the 9Marks series, are designed to help you think through some of life's big questions.

1. GOD: Is He Out There?

2. WAR: Why Did Life Just Get Harder?

3. VOICES: Who Am I Listening To?

4. BIBLE: Can We Trust It?

5. BELIEVE: What Should I Know?

6. CHARACTER: How Do I Change?

7. TRAINING: How Do I Grow As A Christian?

8. CHURCH: Do I Have To Go?

9. RELATIONSHIPS: How Do I Make Things Right?

10. SERVICE: How Do I Give Back?

IX 9Marks

Building Healthy Churches

9Marks exists to equip church leaders with a biblical vision and practical resources for displaying God's glory to the nations through healthy churches.

To that end, we want to see churches characterized by these nine marks of health:

1   Expositional Preaching
2   Biblical Theology
3   A Biblical Understanding of the Gospel
4   A Biblical Understanding of Conversion
5   A Biblical Understanding of Evangelism
6   Biblical Church Membership
7   Biblical Church Discipline
8   Biblical Discipleship
9   Biblical Church Leadership

Find more titles at

www.9Marks.org

20schemes
Gospel Churches for Scotland's Poorest

20schemes exists to bring gospel hope to Scotland's poorest communities through the revitalisation and planting of healthy, gospel-preaching churches, ultimately led by a future generation of indigenous church leaders.

> 'If we are really going to see a turnaround in the lives of residents in our poorest communities, then we have to embrace a radical and long-term strategy which will bring gospel-hope to untold thousands.'
>
> **MEZ McCONNELL,** Ministry Director

We believe that building healthy churches in Scotland's poorest communities will bring true, sustainable, and long-term renewal to countless lives.

THE NEED IS URGENT

Learn more about our work and how to partner with us at:

20SCHEMES.COM
TWITTER.COM/20SCHEMES
FACEBOOK.COM/20SCHEMES
INSTAGRAM.COM/20SCHEMES

Christian Focus Publications

Our mission statement —

STAYING FAITHFUL

In dependence upon God we seek to impact the world through literature faithful to His infallible Word, the Bible. Our aim is to ensure that the Lord Jesus Christ is presented as the only hope to obtain forgiveness of sin, live a useful life and look forward to heaven with Him.

Our books are published in four imprints:

CHRISTIAN
FOCUS

Popular works including biographies, commentaries, basic doctrine and Christian living.

CHRISTIAN
HERITAGE

Books representing some of the best material from the rich heritage of the church.

MENTOR

Books written at a level suitable for Bible College and seminary students, pastors, and other serious readers. The imprint includes commentaries, doctrinal studies, examination of current issues and church history.

CF4•K

Children's books for quality Bible teaching and for all age groups: Sunday school curriculum, puzzle and activity books; personal and family devotional titles, biographies and inspirational stories — because you are never too young to know Jesus!

Christian Focus Publications Ltd,
Geanies House, Fearn, Ross-shire,
IV20 1TW, Scotland, United Kingdom.
www.christianfocus.com